Who Cares for Animals?

Who Cares for Animals?

ANTONY BROWN

Published on behalf of the
Royal Society for the
Prevention of Cruelty to Animals

HEINEMANN : LONDON

William Heinemann Ltd
15 Queen St, Mayfair, London W1X 8BE

LONDON MELBOURNE TORONTO
JOHANNESBURG AUCKLAND

Filmset and printed Offset Litho in England by
Cox and Wyman Ltd, London, Fakenham and Reading

Foreword

by the Chairman of the RSPCA

It is a real pleasure for me to commend this book, not only to members of the RSPCA, but in particular to many people outside the Society who believe that to care for animals is an essential part of any truly civilized nation. I have felt for some time that the RSPCA has had one obvious weakness – its failure to communicate to the public at large the great size and scope of its day-to-day work. The scope is as big as the animal kingdom itself – not just the domestic pet, but the farm animal, the badger or the fox injured on the road, the oiled seabird, and a million travellers through our Airport Hostel. As we become involved with conservation, so we are taking positive steps to befriend the seal and the whale.

I believe that Antony Brown has been successful in a truly remarkable way in capturing not only the fascinating history of the Society, but in bringing the reader a living picture of the work today. Because its development in the tough and callous period of the Industrial Revolution is of singular interest, it must have been tempting for him to concentrate on the nineteeenth century, but the author has firmly decided that the work of today is equally exciting. When reading this book I am sure you will feel yourself getting involved in all our problems, in just the way that Antony Brown has so clearly done.

The story is written not only because it is our 150th Anniversary in 1974, but to show how the world of animal welfare is changing and how little we can rest on past achievements. Certainly, the modern Society with its specialist committees, national corps of Inspectors, and world-wide influence is a very far cry from the days when the Revd. Arthur Broome paid a single Inspector to check the cruelties in Smithfield Market. The old brutality is passing but is being replaced by the less obvious suffering of the battery hen and the veal calves – far more difficult to counter because hidden from the public eye.

It is sometimes said that in a world of human suffering, the distress of animals should have less call on us. It is, I believe, wrong to suppose that there is a conflict between helping people and helping animals. Certainly it is not one which would have occurred to the founders of the Society – to William Wilberforce, for example, whose sensitivity to the sufferings of animals was but the other side of the coin of his concern for human welfare. Today this wider perspective of compassion is one we can see more clearly, as more and more young people react with justifiable anger to the outrages done to people, to animals, and to the environment in general. Yet such concern is not enough if we merely react against the harrying of some rare and interesting species. In all such protests, I believe, the Society can play an increasing part by adding the dimension of compassion.

I am glad the book contains a special account of one difficult and dangerous rescue because people can so easily take for granted the courage of our Inspectors and Clinic Staff. Climbing a 50 foot tree in a high wind with rotten branches snapping under you, to rescue a terrified kitten, or inching your way down a disused culvert on your back in sewage mud to reach an injured dog is not a job for the squeamish. When I read our rescue reports, I marvel at people's cold-blooded bravery. On the occasions when I have been personally involved, I have realized that it is the intense satisfaction of saving a life, together with the knowledge that you could not live with yourself if you had gone home and left the job unfinished.

I am also glad that the author has described in some detail the vastly important work of our branches. The voluntary workers are the backbone of the Society, without whom the whole organization would crumble. They are also the grass roots from which the Council draws its strength. The Society has developed over the years as a middle-of-the-road body and it would soon lead to disaster if the working representatives of our branches lost their place on the Council to the more extreme elements, who in their enthusiasm tend to lose the credibility which is so vital if we are to retain public esteem and Parliamentary influence.

Finally, one short story of my own. A rough-coated sheepdog was being led very nervously along a street in a South Wales town towards the destruction yard, when a young couple drove past in their car, stopped, got out and asked a few questions, lifted the little bitch into the car and drove on. 'Mouse', as we called her, taught my wife and myself how deep can be the world of love for a dog. I often wonder how many other people's lives get changed by a single incident such as this.

JOHN HOBHOUSE

Preface

Although this book has been written for the 150th anniversary
of the Royal Society for the Prevention of Cruelty to Animals, it
has not been my primary aim to write a history. For one thing,
the historical field has already been admirably covered in Mr.
A. W. Moss's book *Valiant Crusade*, published in 1961. Second,
and perhaps more important, one thing became clear to me as
soon as I began my researches – the fact that very few people in
Britain know what the RSPCA really does. From the Inspectors
in the field to the work of its scientific committees, the Society
represents the most powerful agency in the world for animal
welfare. Yet in essence it remains a relatively small group of
dedicated people. It is of these people and their work that I have
tried to draw a living portrait.

One point is worth noting from the start, and that is that
through its long history the Society has in one sense had a double
purpose. 'When a man protects an animal from ill-treatment,'
said the Duke of Windsor at the Society's centenary in 1924,
'his kindly deed reacts upon his own character and makes him a
better citizen. In contemplating what the RSPCA is doing for
animals we should not lose sight of the humanizing effect of its
work on the hearts of the community.' Today, the humanizing
effect is more than ever needed. If Richard Martin, Arthur
Broome, and William Wilberforce could come back today they
would not see bull-baiting, or exhausted horses being whipped
through the streets of London. The modern age deals in less
obvious brutalities, of which the reader will find many examples
in this book. On the credit side he will also find some account of
what the RSPCA is doing to combat them.

Any book of this kind must be in a real sense a collaboration
between an author and his subject, and my work would have been
impossible without the kindness and co-operation of many people
mentioned in these pages. I am greatly indebted to Mr. John
Hobhouse, the Chairman of the Society, for his constant
encouragement and help, and for the many hours he has given up
to discussing the smallest details as well as the broadest issues.
Many members of the RSPCA Council have been most helpful
to me, but I must especially thank Mrs. Angela Cope and Mrs.
Peggy Tait for giving me the benefit of their great knowledge and
enthusiasm for the Society. Professor John Napier and Mr.
Frederick Burden, M.P., have been particularly helpful on the
stories of factory farming and the SELFA campaign respectively:
and I must thank Mr. Richard Ryder for talking to me about

many aspects of the Society apart from his own special interest of animal experimentation. Mrs. Ruth Harrison has been an invaluable guide on factory farming, and her book, *Animal Machines*, has contributed powerfully to many people's thinking, my own included.

Among members of the Headquarters staff I must particularly thank Major Ronald Seager for his kind and courteous help on my many visits to Horsham. To Mr. Mike Seymour-Rouse I owe a special debt for his guidance, encouragement, and not least his tolerance at many stages of my work. I would also like to thank Mr. Clive Willis for many talks on various aspects of the Society's work, and Mrs. Barbara Escott for her help with the photographs. At the same time I must stress that the Publicity Department are in no way responsible for the views expressed in this book. Indeed, it is a measure of the collective strength of the RSPCA that I have been encouraged to describe the Society as I saw it. No organization can thrive without the dynamic of discussion and sometimes disagreement: where such differences exist, as on the question of fox-hunting, it has been my aim to present all views with sympathy and, I hope, with fairness.

Among members of the Horsham staff not mentioned elsewhere, I must also thank Major Langham, Mr. John Douglass, and Mr. Richard Sayer. Chief Superintendent Butfield of the Inspectorate has on many occasions found time to give me the benefit not only of his experience but his enthusiasm. Finally I must thank my secretary, Diana Cookson, for her patience and helpfulness as usual.

Sutton Valence, Kent   ANTONY BROWN

Contents

The Way They Should Be

'You see those two Red Admirals? That's why we don't cut down the nettles.' John Goodman, the warden at Mallydam's Wood, lowered his binoculars and pointed. Around us were sixty acres of Sussex woodland, deep glades where insects clustered in the sunlight. The two Red Admirals rose and fluttered like helicopters round the nettles.

'You mean the butterflies like them?'

'Red Admirals do.' The warden nodded. 'If you want Red Admirals in the garden, don't cut down your nettles.'

Preserving nettles, I suggested, seemed an odd role for the RSPCA.

The warden laughed, and said that you couldn't really separate one bit of nature from another. Then he led the way over to a small collection of runs and cages. Apart from being a woodland reserve, he explained, Mallydam's Wood was a small sanctuary for wild creatures that local people brought in injured. 'You get a badger that's been hit by a car, a fox cub found abandoned.' In one of the cages there was an owl that the warden said he wasn't very happy about: he thought it had got some brain damage from a road accident, and would most likely have to be put down. The kestrel in the next cage had had something wrong with his eye, but was nearly cured and would soon be going.

'Do you mind when they go?'

'Mind?' John Goodman looked a bit surprised. 'What we mind is when we have to keep them. We want them to be free. For a wild creature it's the way they should be.'

The way they should be. The words were to come back to me often in the next few months. Many times while writing this book I was to see how animals should not be – the polluted seabirds on the Cornish coast, the factory calves living out brief lives in darkness, the stray unwanted dogs of Liverpool. Now, as the warden spoke, I remembered a little spider monkey I had seen, a few days before, on a seaside pier where a beach photographer kept him chained to his shoulder to pose with holiday makers. Miserable and pathetic-looking on his chain, his life had seemed not so much a cruelty as a lie.

I told him about the monkey and he nodded. 'If I can make a suggestion about this book you're going to write. The RSPCA's not just about preventing cruelty. It's also about respect. Respect for the world around us. Isn't man in danger of losing his own roots if he loses touch with the natural world? You could even say that if we don't keep animals the way they should be, we end by damaging ourselves.'

The way they should be. Or, if you went into it deep enough: the way *we* should be.

In a sense, it was to be the theme of everything that followed.

1 : The Mutual Bond

'Unto men we owe Justice, and to all other creatures that
are capable of it, grace and benignity. There is a kinde of
interchangeable commerce and mutuall bond betweene
them and us.'

Montaigne

Man, the Master

One of the most remarkable discoveries of modern times happened
because a young French boy lost his dog. The boy's name was Ravidat
and he lived near Montignac in the valley of the Dordogne River.
One evening in September 1940 Ravidat with four friends and his
little dog Robot set off in the direction of a hill known locally as
Lascaux. Presently one of them noticed that Robot was missing. They
started to look for him, then heard barking coming from the hill of
Lascaux.

Ravidat and his friends found that there was a hole, made by the fall
of a big fir-tree. Ravidat clambered through the hole – then fell twenty
feet on to the slippery floor of a cave. He found Robot unharmed, then
noticed something else.

He struck a match, called to his friends to come down, then stared
round. The wall of the cave was covered with paintings – bulls, bison,
reindeer, horses, and men with spears, glowing yellow in the darkness.
Ravidat and his friends lit match after match. What the little dog's
fall had led them to was the finest example of palaeolithic cave art
ever seen – the work of hunters who had lived in the Dordogne valley
fifteen thousand years before.

You may be wondering what Robot's discovery has to do with the
theme of this book. The point about the Lascaux cave-paintings is
that they give us the first glimpse of how primitive man saw the world
around him. Palaeolithic man was still a hunter. Many thousands of
years before, his earliest ancestor had taken the decisive step of standing
upright, then gone on to develop his brain and his hands. Even in
palaeolithic times, man still lived on the same terms as the animals –

Mallydams Wood. Sixty acres of Sussex woodland make
a sanctuary for wild or injured creatures.

they had their lairs, he had his cave. When it came to the hunt for food
or possession of the land, the bison, bull, and mammoth were still his
rivals.

If we look closely at reproductions of the Lascaux paintings what we
feel most strongly is the artist's sense of awe. The men are weak and
puny, almost like cartoon figures, while the beasts are huge and

powerful. It is they, you feel, who are masters of the forest – not man with his tiny armoury of flints and spearheads.

Now let us imagine more millennia passing. Palaeolithic times have given way to neolithic. Somewhere around 8000 B.C., man's relation with the animal world has undergone a decisive change – he is no longer merely a hunter. With the increasing skill of his hands and brain he has become first a herdsman, then a farmer. Sometimes he may still hunt the deer and the wild boar, but he no longer has the feeling of awe his ancestors felt in the Lascaux caves, for he has learnt to control the beasts. On his farms there will be pigs, goats, and oxen. By his fireside his children may even play with the dog he keeps for rounding up the sheep.

As he looks at the world around him, man will often be impressed by the beauty and strength of the animals. But his first thought will be how they can serve him.

Now that he has such power, how is he going to use it?

*

'If you want Red Admirals don't cut down your nettles.'

The farmer of primitive times knew, as any hill-farmer will tell you today, that if a cow or a sheep is to thrive it must also be well cared for. Scattered among the books of the Old Testament we find the first sketchy beginnings of the rules of good husbandry. Most often they are a mixture of humanity and common sense. The ox must not be muzzled when he treads the corn – in other words he is to be allowed to pick up a few bits for himself while working. Another rule says that if your brother's ox or his sheep go astray you must help him to find them. An ox and an ass must not be yoked together – the point being that two animals of unequal size not only put a strain on each other, but plough an uneven furrow.

Sometimes, more rarely, there are examples of what might be called uncalculated kindness. If you find a mother bird sitting on a nest, says the Book of Deuteronomy, you must leave her and not try to catch her. Nor must you boil a kid in its mother's milk.

Such gestures might soften man's relation to the animal world, but they did not change it. For had not God, in the Book of Genesis, ordained that man should have the mastery of all creation? 'And God said unto them, Be fruitful, and multiply and replenish the earth, and subdue it; and have dominion over the fish of the sea, and over the birds of the heavens, and over every living thing that moveth upon the earth.' To the Israelite farmers in their tents in Samaria and by the banks of Jordan, the words must have seemed both a commandment and a promise.

Yet it was not the only view of man's relation with the animal kingdom. In Zoroastrianism, the religion of Ancient Persia, we find far more emphasis on the idea that animals, as well as men, are created by God. Much of the teaching is in a kind of poetic hymn known as the Avesti. In one passage there is an ox who complains that he receives bad treatment from man, whereon Zarathustra, the god, undertakes to protect him.

In some early civilizations you feel that man is seeing animals not merely as something to be used, but almost as a clue to the mystery of his own existence. In Ancient Egypt, a temple would often have its special sacred animal. Cats, crocodiles, even vultures would be embalmed and treated with great honour after their death. Pythagoras, in Ancient Greece, believed in the transmigration of souls, by which the spirits of dead people were believed to be contained in animals, and vice versa. The Pythagoreans taught kindness to animals, but not necessarily for the animals' own sake – you must not beat a dog, they said, because in its howls you might hear the voice of a dead person you had known.

4

In the great Eastern religions we find a much stronger sense of reverence for life. The essence of this view is a sense that some particle of the divine nature exists in every aspect of creation. Thus it is wrong to destroy or damage life even in its humblest form. In India a Jain monk must carry a broom to brush insects out of the road where he is walking, and strain even a glass of water in case he swallows some minute creature.

Jainism has much in common with Buddhism. No Buddhist is allowed to take life, for he believes in the transmigration of souls, and the spirit contained in the body of an ant may be on its way to a higher form of life. One of the first practical humane reformers we know of was a Buddhist – Asoka, King of Maghada in North India in the third century B.C., who abolished sacrificial slaughter in his kingdom, banned the royal hunt, and planted mango trees, to give shade to man and beast.

If we look to see what was happening to animals in Europe at the same time, we find a brutal and a bloody contrast. In the two centuries before the birth of Christ the gladiatorial contests of Ancient Rome were at their height. While King Asoka was planting his mango trees in Asia, the arenas of Ancient Rome ran with the blood of lions, elephants, not to mention such gentle creatures as the ostrich and the giraffe. In one day, at the opening of the Games in the reign of Titus, five thousand beasts were slaughtered.

Probably the spectators were case-hardened rather than cruel. No doubt they would have told you that they went to the arena to watch the skill of the gladiators, the ritual of the occasion, or because they had always done so. Cruelty, in our own time as in Ancient Rome, is largely a matter of acquiescence.

But the story of humane reform is, above all, the story of those who refused to acquiesce. Even in the heyday of Imperial Rome there were a handful of such spirits. There was Cicero, who asked what pleasure an educated man could have in seeing a fine animal run through with a spear? There was Plutarch, the historian, who would not allow his old oxen to be slaughtered but put them out to grass instead. Years ahead of his time, he wrote pamphlets attacking not only hunting but the practice of starving animals before their death to make the meat taste better. The most civilized minds in Rome might see animals as an inferior creation. It did not, in their eyes, reduce the need for justice. 'Since justice is due to rational beings', wrote the philosopher Porphyry, 'how is it possible to evade the assumption that we are bound also to act justly towards the races below us?'

It is one of the odd paradoxes of the story that when we come to Christianity we find almost no reference to the treatment of animals. True, there are the ox and the ass in the stable, there is the donkey on which Christ rode into Jerusalem, and continually we find the tender imagery of the Good Shepherd and his sheep. Yet nowhere in the New Testament is there a specific injunction to be kind to animals. It was left to Francis of Assisi, more than a thousand years later, to redress the balance.

But even if animals did not have souls, they could be held responsible for their actions. Nothing in the story of man's inhumanity is more grotesque than the animal trials which took place in the ecclesiastical courts of the Middle Ages. Based on a verse from the Book of Exodus which said an ox which had gored a person must be stoned, the practice of trying animals spread all over Europe. Few records survive, but it seems certain that thousands of pigs, dogs, and bullocks were tried and put to death. Sometimes, it is true, an animal might be acquitted – perhaps the oddest twist to the proceedings was that an accused animal had the same rights as a human. He actually appeared in the dock, and was defended by counsel who might persuade the judge to let him off. In England the bizarre practice went on till 1771, when a dog was tried at Chichester in Sussex.

But the trials of animals were humane compared with what happened in the name of sport. Even so sensitive a spirit as Sir Thomas More was said to excel in the game of cock-throwing, which consisted of throwing sticks at a bird tied to a post. The game ended with the cockerel's death, but to make it more difficult, grease would be smeared on the feathers so that the sticks flicked off. On Shrove Tuesday, wrote a humanely minded French observer in the fourteenth century, 'the English eat a certain cake, upon which they immediately run mad and kill their poor cocks.'

A much older tradition was that of bull-baiting. The bull was tethered to a metal ring, then attacked by specially trained dogs whose role was to bite the bull's nose, so long as they could avoid being tossed by it: the bull was further tormented by having pepper blown up through his nostrils. In the town of Stamford there was an annual festival which involved the pursuit of an enraged bull through the town by dogs. This time-honoured ritual had begun in King John's time, and actually survived long enough to be suppressed by the RSPCA, in one of its earliest prosecutions, in 1837. Other so-called sports involved monkeys, bears and badgers, but the most traditional of all was cock-fighting, which A. W. Moss records as dating from 1400 B.C. In the cock-fight, metal spurs were put on the gamecock, which would have had its comb and tail feathers trimmed, to reduce the chance of its opponent gaining hold. Both birds would fight on till one, or sometimes both, died either of wounds or of exhaustion.

As we read such accounts we might well feel that the whole medieval world was a kind of bloody arena for both man and beast. Yet it was not greatly worse than what had gone before, or what would follow.

Here and there the murky medieval sky is lit by some brief flare of enlightenment or pity. There was St. Giles, the patron saint of cripples, whose own disability had come from helping a wounded hind. St. Jerome lived in the desert with a lion and a lamb for companions – the lion had become his friend when he had extracted a thorn from its foot, like Androcles in the legend. In Britain itself there was St. Monacella of Wales, who shielded a hare from the pursuers' arrows with her robe, and St. Cuthbert, who was said to have such power over animals that otters would come and play at his feet, and then receive his blessing. In the chronicles of the medieval Church there is even a touching cardinal who allowed mice and rats to bite him. Since they had no souls, he said, they had no prospects of pleasure in the next world, and might as well enjoy themselves in this.

But the figure who really illuminates the Middle Ages is St. Francis. Born the son of a tradesman in Assisi, Francisco Bernardone gave up his youthful dreams of military glory to become a monk. One day he exchanged clothes with a beggar, and went to work in a hospital for lepers. Later he founded his own Order: the Franciscans, as they came to be known, lived in huts or in the open and wore the coarse brown tunic of Italian peasants. St. Francis used to preach to the birds and called all animals his brothers. Once a fisherman gave him a large fish he had caught. St. Francis courteously thanked him, took the fish, and put it back in the water, bidding it bless God.

When he was going to preach to the birds, he used to listen to them singing first, then wait till their noise subsided. 'Little sisters,' he would say, 'if you have now had your say, it is fit I should also be heard', on which the birds would all fall silent. Such anecdotes might be thought to suggest the archetype of a sentimental animal-lover, but nothing could be less true of St. Francis. Like all great humane reformers, there were no priorities in his compassion. 'It was like a deep tide', says G. K. Chesterton, 'driving out to uncharted seas of charity.'

St. Francis had done more than anyone to bring a concern for animals within the Christian faith. Now, as the centuries went by, the pendulum of intellectual opinion swung back and forth. In 1637 the French philosopher Descartes argued that animals had no souls or feelings.

7

Another view came from the great French essayist, Montaigne, who said that it was only through man's vanity

> that he dare equall himselfe to God, that he ascribeth divine conditions unto himselfe that he selecteth and separateth himselfe from out the ranke of other creatures . . . How knoweth he by the vertue of his understanding the inward and secret motions of beasts? By what comparison from them to us doth he conclude the brutishnesse, he ascribeth unto them? When I am playing with my Cat, who knowes whether she have more sport in dallying with me, than I have in gaming with her? . . . It is a matter of divination to guesse in whom the fault is, that we understand not one another. For we understand them no more than they us. By the same reason, may they as well esteem us beasts . . .

No writer before Montaigne had so sharply questioned man's superiority, and no later writer would ever define his obligation with such breadth and vision. 'Unto men we owe Justice, and to all other creatures that are capable of it, grace and benignity', he wrote. 'There is a kinde of inter-changeable commerce and mutuall bond betweene them and us.'

Another two centuries were to pass before the mutual bond would be acknowledged.

The Making of the Law

We move forward to the England of George III: as it greeted the nineteenth century, how were the animals faring? In London, says A. W. Moss:

> it was no unusual happening for a horse to be beaten to death; whilst bull-baiting, bear-baiting and cock-fighting had again become popular entertainment in towns and villages alike. Fights were arranged between dogs and cats, or dogs and monkeys, and a delighted audience roared its approval as the stronger of the two animals tore his adversary to pieces and stood triumphant over a mangled heap of blood and fur. Cattle, sheep and pigs brought to London for slaughter were killed in underground cellars, the sheep being literally thrown out of the carts, where the animals lay bruised and injured for days at a time, until finally put out of their misery by the slaughterer's knife. Calves were strung up, their mouths taped to still their cries, and were slowly bled to death.

8

On the face of it, things were as bad as anything in Imperial Rome, but there was something to be set against such horrors. This was the awakening conscience of England. It is one of the more fortunate rules of progress that any thrusting and ebullient society always tends to produce its critics and dissenters.

Something of the kind had begun to happen in eighteenth-century England. Beginning with George Fox and the Quakers, and continuing with the Methodists, a new spirit had begun to colour the views of generous-minded people. They saw themselves surrounded – and in some cases materially enriched – by a society which permitted slavery, cruelty to children, and which amused itself by torturing animals. 'Something better remains after death for these poor creatures also', said John Wesley, and there must have been many who came to hear him preach in the Cornish quarries and the Midlands meadows who felt their consciences stirred.

Nor was it only the Methodists. The Church broke its long silence on animal cruelty, and from the country rectories of England, there began a steady trickle of books and pamphlets. In 1768 the Revd. Richard Dean produced *An Essay on the Future Life of Brute Creatures*. Four years later the Revd. James Granger of Shiplake in Oxfordshire wrote an article denouncing the ill-treatment of horses used by draymen. When he preached on the same theme from his village pulpit he was denounced as a madman by his parishioners, who had to be soothed down by his bishop.

Secular support came, as always, from the artists and writers, among them Blake and Cowper. Hogarth produced a series of cartoons called 'Four Stages of Cruelty' which was sold in thousands. If his pictures had the effect of checking cruelty to dumb animals, he said, then he would be prouder than if he had painted Raphael's Cartoons.

So we begin to get the beginnings of a unity which would be a basis for reform – but now, for the first time, there was something else. In the past, as we have seen, individuals had often urged greater kindness. But what nobody had ever suggested was that cruelty should actually be banned by law. Now, in a book by Jeremy Bentham, there came the first hint that this might one day happen:

Why should the law refuse its protection to any sensitive being? The time will come when humanity will extend its mantle over everything which breathes. We have begun by attending to the condition of slaves; we shall finish by softening that of all the animals which assist our labours or supply our wants.

Cock-fighting. Though Samuel Pepys thought it 'no great sport'
in the seventeenth century, it remained popular till the nineteenth.

Jeremy Bentham's book had been published in 1780 – exactly two
centuries after the first publication in France of Montaigne's *Essays*.
And now, as England moved into the new century, there came the first
attempt to secure legislation to protect animals from cruelty. In April
1800 a courageous M.P. named Sir William Pulteney sought leave to
bring in a Bill to prevent bull-baiting.

Such an aim might seem to us moderate enough, yet so strong was
the attachment of Georgian England to what it saw as its liberties
that it was hotly contested in the Commons. The opposition was led
by Windham, the Secretary of State for War. Among Windham's
supporters was at least one future Prime Minister, George Canning,
who declared in the debate that 'the amusement inspired courage and
produced a nobleness of sentiment and elevation of mind'.

Sheridan also spoke in the debate, but in support of the Bill, declaring
bull-baiting to be a 'cowardly, beastly, execrable practice' and com-

paring it unfavourably with the new sport of cricket. On the division the Bill was lost by two votes, much to the approval of *The Times*, which pronounced that any law which interfered with how a man spent his leisure was tyranny.

But the narrow defeat of Sir William Pulteney's Bill had given the reformers new heart. In June 1809 a new Bill was drawn up to prevent malicious or wanton cruelty in general. This time it was presented by somebody with whom even Canning and *The Times* would have to reckon – Lord Erskine of Restormel, Lord Chancellor and perhaps the most distinguished lawyer of the day. Erskine was not only an eminent man, but a deeply humane one. The story was told of him that once on Hampstead Heath he came across a man beating his horse. When Erskine rebuked him, the man gave the favourite answer of all who ill-use their animals.

Lord Erskine of Restormel, 1750–1823.
His Bill to prevent malicious cruelty to
animals was greeted in Parliament
with derision.

11

'Can't I do what I like with my own?'

'Yes', replied Erskine. 'And so can I. This stick is my own.' Upon which England's leading lawyer administered a thoroughly non-judicial thrashing.

Such anecdotes are not merely picturesque. They illustrate something which it is important to understand about the reform movement. Englishmen really *did* feel that it was important for a man to be able to beat a horse if it was his own property – it was one of the bastions of his liberty. Because of this, the battle over the reform laws involved just such passionate feelings as, for example, the reform of the Abortion Law in our own time.

When Erskine brought his Bill before the House it was at first greeted with derision. However, he managed to secure its passage as far as the second reading. The scope of the Bill covered ill-treatment of horses, sheep and dogs: anyone found guilty of ill-treatment should be liable for up to a month's imprisonment. The Bill was defeated at its second reading, but this time the press, at least, had changed its tune. There was support from the *Gentleman's Magazine* which said that 'few subjects in the whole compass of moral discussion can be greater than the unnecessary cruelty of man to animals'. Even *The Times*, perhaps more impressed by Lord Erskine's position than by his ideas on reform, this time expressed its 'humble appreciation of the author of the Bill', and went on to applaud the idea of 'a system of rights and privileges even for the mute and unconscious part of creation'.

Meanwhile the first really positive step was now about to come. If the 'mute and unconscious part of creation' had only known, there might now have gone out from the slaughter-houses and the cock-pits and the cat-skinning yards and the wretched sheds and stalls where animals suffered all over England, such a roaring and barking and huzzaing as had never been heard in the animal kingdom.

For they had found a new champion. His name was Richard Martin.

*

It is a popular canard that people concerned with animal welfare are by nature sentimental. The kind of people who worry about ill-treated cats and dogs, according to this view, remain blithely indifferent to starving children. In fact such a version is seldom if ever true, for compassion is indivisible, and the history of humane reform shows that those most sensitive to animal suffering are usually even more so to the suffering of humans.

Nobody bears this out more than Richard Martin, the author of the first successful Parliamentary Bill to limit cruelty. Martin also helped to abolish such medieval horrors as capital punishment for forgery. He was a pioneer of contemporary moves to provide free legal aid for those who could not afford it. On his Irish estate he provided work and homes for orphan children, and even built a model prison so that local wrong-doers were not sent away from home.

Nor was he anything like the conventional picture of a social reformer. Born in Dublin in 1754, he was brought up with all the extravagant panache of eighteenth-century Ireland. He had a passion for duelling, and in his youth acquired the nickname of 'Hairtrigger Dick'. Once he faced a howling mob armed with a tiny pistol, and so charmed them with his style and courage that they ended up by giving him three cheers.

After being educated in the traditional mode of Harrow and Cambridge, Martin qualified as a barrister but scarcely ever practised. Indeed, as heir to a 200,000 acre estate, he scarcely needed to. He represented Galway in the House of Commons where he was known for his Irish brogue and wit; his views may sometimes have been thought eccentric but he was what the House of Commons loves, a card. Once King George IV visited Ireland during election time and inquired of Martin which candidate would be returned. 'The survivor, Sir', said Martin.

Another time an old opponent happened to pass him in St. James's Street. In those days it was a matter of courtesy to allow somebody else to pass on the inside of the pavement, where they would be less likely to get splashed with mud from passing carriages.

'I never give the wall to a blackguard', said Martin's opponent, pushing past.

Martin stepped aside. 'I always do', he said, bowing low.

What made this urbane and sophisticated Irishman take up the cause of animal welfare? His ruling force seems to have been straightforward generosity – mixed with a streak of combativeness as well. In his youth he once fought a duel with a man who had killed a wolfhound. To the end of his days, he would inspect the horses drawing a stage-coach, and if one of them was suffering, would order the coachman to take it out of the shafts. In the House of Commons, twenty years earlier, he had supported Sir William Pulteney's Bill.

Even so, we know nothing of the circumstances which made him decide to try a new Bill of his own. Entitled 'A Bill to prevent the cruel and improper treatment of cattle', it was first presented to the House on 1 June 1821.

Richard Martin, 1754–1834, Member of Parliament
for Galway. George IV nicknamed him 'Humanity
Dick' because of his work for animals.

Because it was so important in its effect, the Bill itself is worth looking at in a little detail. 'If any person or persons', it said,

> having the charge care or custody of any horse, cow, ox, heifer, steer,
> sheep or other cattle, the property of any other person or persons, shall
> wantonly beat, abuse or ill-treat any such animal, such individuals
> shall be brought before a justice of the peace or other magistrate.

If politics is the art of the possible, Martin's was an adept exercise.
For once, he had restrained his natural exuberance and limited himself
to strict objectives. The Bill, as drawn up, applied only to cattle and
other farm animals: if it had included cats and dogs, Martin knew, it
would have been far less likely to have been passed. In the same way
it only specified people *in charge of* animals, not their owners. Thus the

14

The first meeting at Old Slaughter's. This plaque
stood on the corner of St. Martin's Lane and
Cranbourn Street till the demolition
of the coffee house.

William Wilberforce, 1759–1833. When he had freed the slaves
he turned his attention to the sufferings of animals.

Englishman's supposedly sacred right to do what he liked with his own property was not infringed.

Such cool drafting was to be well rewarded. Apart from a few laborious Members' jokes about asses being included, the House gave it an easy passage by 48 votes to 16. Then, on going to the Lords, it was defeated. The next year Martin presented the Bill a second time when, thanks to the skilful steering of Lord Erskine in the Lords, it was finally passed, and received the Royal Assent on 22 July 1822. Hair-trigger Dick acquired a new nickname, Humanity Dick – bestowed, it was said, by George IV himself.

Thus the first ridge had been scaled. Beyond it lay far greater peaks of cruelty. But meanwhile how far would the new law be actually observed? Even if the hard-pressed police found time to prosecute, would any but a few liberal-minded magistrates risk unpopularity by sentencing offenders? That was the question which now faced the reformers.

Divers Benevolent Persons

'Whereas in the year one thousand eight hundred and twenty-four at Old Slaughter's Coffee House Saint Martin's Lane in the city of Westminster a society for the prevention of cruelty to animals was established by divers benevolent persons . . .'

So runs the wording of the RSPCA's Act of Incorporation. And certainly the event it commemorates is the most significant in the story of animal welfare. Old Slaughter's Coffee House, long since demolished, stood on the corner of St. Martin's Lane and Cranbourn St. in London. Its name, nothing to do with slaughter-houses, was merely that of the original proprietor. All the same, the irony could hardly have been lost on the company who met on the evening of 16 June 1824.

Even from the scanty records that survive, we can tell that it was a distinguished gathering. In the chair was Fowell Buxton, M.P., one of the famous family of Quakers and a brother-in-law of Elizabeth Fry, the prison reformer. With him were several colleagues from the Commons. One was Richard Martin, and among the others was a tall, gentle-looking man whose arrival must have caused more than a murmur of interest, for everyone knew William Wilberforce, the man who, nearly twenty years before, had ended slavery in the British Colonies. But it is unlikely that anybody in that fashionable part of London would have known the man who had actually called the meeting – the Revd. Arthur Broome, vicar of the extremely unfashionable parish of St. Mary's, at Bromley in East London.

To the group who met in St. Martin's Lane, Broome was already known as an active worker for humane reform. Indeed, two years before, he had called a similar meeting at Old Slaughter's: he was trying to form a society which would support the working of Richard Martin's Act against cruelty to cattle. Apparently this project had failed to get off the ground, but Broome had not ceased his efforts.

One thing in particular he had done in the intervening period was to be prophetic. Paying him out of his own pocket, he had employed a man named Wheeler to watch for cases of cruelty which could be punished under Martin's Act.

This time, unlike the previous meeting at Old Slaughter's, progress was evidently made. In the Minute Book, which is still preserved, we read that two committees were appointed. One was to superintend 'the Publication of Tracts, Sermons, and similar modes of influencing public opinion'. The other had the more immediately practical aim of 'Inspecting the Markets and Streets of the Metropolis, the Slaughter Houses, and the conduct of Coachmen'. In the Minutes the Society is not specifically named, but is described as 'instituted for the purpose of preventing Cruelty to Animals'.

The first animal welfare society in any country now officially existed.

It is worth noting that Richard Martin, at the first meeting, stressed that it should not primarily exist to prosecute offenders. It would be ill-judged, he said, for it to become known as a prosecuting society, and the prime aim should be 'to alter the moral feelings of the country'. Over the following century and a half, his words were to be prophetic.

Despite Martin's contribution, the moving spirit among the founders was clearly Arthur Broome. Within four days of the first meeting, at which he had been appointed Secretary, he had called the first meeting of the committee appointed to deal with publications. Probably as a result of his own persuasion, he was able to report that the rector of Marylebone had undertaken to preach a sermon against cruelty. There is also a mention of what seems to have been the first donation, anonymously, of £50. A week later another committee meeting was called, and it was agreed that the Society should print and distribute tracts, presumably paid for with the £50. Among the tracts was one about bull-baiting, by a Mrs. Hall, who seems to have been the first woman associated with the new Society.

For the next two years there is a gap in our knowledge of the Society's activities. But active it must have been, for by 1826, it was in debt to the tune of just on £300. Arthur Broome seems to have financed much of the work himself – in the first three years he had paid bills amounting to £67 from his own pocket, and was owed another £13 by the Society.

The situation was somewhat improved by the bequest of £100 from the estate of Mrs. Radcliffe, the highly successful author of *The Mysteries of Udolpho*, but it was evidently not enough. Broome had already resigned the living of St. Mary's, Bromley, to devote himself full-time to the Society. Now, at a meeting in January 1826, we read that another member of the committee 'was appointed honorary secretary *pro tem* in the absence of Mr. Broome'. The reason for the founder's absence, which did not figure in the minutes, was that Arthur Broome was in jail – arrested because of the Society's debts. Eventually the committee managed to raise enough to secure his release, though not to return the £70 the Society by then owed him.

Meanwhile the first effects of the Society were beginning to be felt. We read of a lady in Ave Maria Lane near St. Paul's being thanked by the committee for 'her humane and zealous exertions to prevent cruelty to a lamb and in giving clear evidence at the Guildhall against the drover who had perpetrated a most wanton and unnecessary cruelty on the same'. One Jeremiah Barrett is similarly thanked for helping to prosecute 'the driver of a cart for having committed an act of wanton cruelty on a horse'.

Obviously such co-operation from the public helped, but something else was more important. This was the beginning of the long tradition of the Society's Inspectors. Arthur Broome, as we saw earlier, had employed a man named Wheeler at his own expense to keep a lookout for cruelty. In 1824, Mr. Wheeler had evidently asked for an assistant, for a man named Charles Teasdall was appointed. We have no exact records of what their duties were, but they seem to have been effective – in the first six months of 1824 they brought sixty-three offenders, mostly from Smithfield Market, before the courts.

What the rate of successful prosecutions was, we do not know. Certainly magistrates were still often hesitant to punish an offender under the 1822 Act. Sometimes Martin himself would bring a prosecution under his own Act: probably the most famous occasion came when he prosecuted a costermonger named Bill Burns for cruelty to a donkey. In the court room it became clear that despite Burns's obvious guilt, the magistrates were not going to convict him. Humanity Dick, with the flair for showmanship that would have made him a superb public relations man in a later age, saw that there was only one thing to do. Without a word to anyone he left the court, returning with the donkey, which he proceeded to lead into the well of the court. Once its wounds were publicly seen, the magistrate had no choice but to

The trial of Bill Burns.

fine Bill Burns. More important, the case was widely talked of and even gave rise to a popular song:

> *If I had a donkey wot wouldn't go,*
> *D'ye think I'd wollop him? No, no, no!*
> *But gentle means I'd try, d'ye see,*
> *Because I hate all cruelty.*
> *If all had been like me, in fact,*
> *There'd ha' been no occasion for Martin's Act.*

Another time Martin sued a coachman flogging his horse in Cheapside: he engaged the cab for himself and took the reins to show the cabman that there were better ways of handling a horse. Subsequently Martin prosecuted the cabman, and then found that the man had only just got the job after being out of work for months. Martin, with a characteristically generous *volte face*, begged the magistrate not to continue with the charge he had brought himself. The magistrate pointed out that under Martin's own law he was bound to convict, but fixed the penalty at the minimum of 10 shillings, which Martin paid himself.

Meanwhile there was still plenty of occasion, not only for Martin's Act, but others like it. Between 1822 and 1826, Humanity Dick himself presented a series of Bills. Among them was one to extend his original Act to include cats and dogs, and another was to remedy the conditions in slaughter-houses. In 1826 he made another attempt to bring in a law to suppress cruel sports, but despite his passionate pleading, all these Bills were defeated. In 1826, the animals' greatest Parliamentary defender lost his seat in the Commons when his opponents protested about what seems to have been a more than usually turbulent Irish election. Martin's supporters were said to have not only voted twice, but to have attacked his opponent's committee rooms. It was never alleged that Martin himself had condoned such practices, but the petition to unseat him was successful. In 1834 he died at Boulogne, where with a typical last flourish of eighteenth-century style, he had gone to escape the creditors to whom his estate was mortgaged. *The Times*, which had never particularly liked the cause of animal welfare, merely recorded the death of 'the late eccentric M.P. for Galway', but a truer verdict came from Thomas Hood:

Thou Wilberforce of hacks!
Of whites as well as blacks,
Piebald and dapple-grey,
Chestnut and bay –
No poet's eulogy thy name adorns,
But oxen from the fens,
Sheep in their pens,
Praise thee, and red cows with winding horns!

Three years later, there came the death of Arthur Broome as well. What we know of him after the founding of the Society is shadowy. He resigned as Secretary in 1828, but still served on the committee, though he does not seem to have attended meetings from then until his death. Reading between the lines, it is impossible not to guess at some disharmony; if so, there was an attempt to patch it up in 1828 when the committee recorded a reference to him as 'the benevolent Founder of the Society . . . whose approbation they should ever deem necessary to all regulations of importance to its objects'.

Little as we know of him, there can be no doubt that Arthur Broome must have the credit for the founding of the RSPCA. There is no record of how he lived in the ten years after he gave up his Bromley living. We know that he died at Birmingham, but not where he is buried, or what he looked like. The only personal thing we know of him is his beautiful handwriting in the Society's Minute Book.

That, and the fact that through his self-effacing efforts the first animal protection society in the world had come to being.

*

Perhaps it takes the death of its pioneers to begin to give respectability to a new movement. In the early days the progress of the Society had been inseparable from Richard Martin's work in Parliament. Now that he was no longer there, there were others to carry on his work. In 1828 a Member named Littleton presented four petitions from Staffordshire against bull-baiting. Sir James Mackintosh, M.P., a founding member of the Society, presented another petition from West Bromwich. Neither was successful, but in the debates the Members for both the cities of Waterford and Wells said that their constituents had now been so roused against bull-baiting that it had been banned in both cities. Slowly, but very surely, the climate of opinion was coming round.

In 1835 there came the first successful Bill since Martin's. Joseph Pease, one of the famous family of Quaker industrialists from the north-east, was a member of the Society's committee. As M.P. for South Durham he introduced a Bill which increased the protection of Martin's Act by including bulls and domestic animals. In effect it improved the conditions in slaughter-houses and, in theory at least, put an end to bull-baiting and cock-fighting. Gradually, and through the now recognized procedure of M.P.s working with the Society, there came a series of small but positive steps. In 1839 the Hackney Carriage Metropolitan Act imposed new rules on drivers relating to the treatment of their horses. Another Act in the same year empowered the Metropolitan Police – but not as yet those throughout the country – to enter premises where they suspected cock-fighting was going on.

Legislation was only one aspect. Now that it had begun to get its financial difficulties sorted out, the Society's influence was spreading. In the summer of 1835 an approach was evidently made to seek Royal support, for a letter arrived from Kensington Palace:

I have laid before the Duchess of Kent your letter of the 2nd inst. and its enclosure, relating to the Society for the Prevention of Cruelty to Animals and Her Royal Highness very readily acceded to your request that her name and that of the Princess Victoria be placed on the list of Lady Patronesses.

For a society whose members had been dismissed as cranks a couple of decades back, it must have seemed impressive recognition. But the main aim was still to see that the hard-won legislation was properly enforced. Springing from that we can begin to see, from the end of the 1830s onwards, the organization of Inspectors in its present form. By 1841 there were five of them, each paid a guinea a week. At this time all Inspectors were based in London: they would be directed, says A. W. Moss

to various parts of the country for temporary duty, then, having brought a number of offenders before the courts, it was evidently thought that this would be a sufficient warning to others. It was a wise scheme when resources were slender and the number of men available was few.

Meanwhile it was obvious that the sytem of London-based Inspectors could only be a beginning. Soon the Society's members at Brighton were wanting a local Inspector. Initiating a practice which has continued since, the local branch was asked to pay £20 a year towards his annual salary. By 1842 Bristol, Bath, Coventry and Scarborough were all wanting Inspectors, and thanks to a series of bequests, including one of £1,000 from a Mrs. Forster, the number was increased from five to ten.

In those times Inspectors often did their job at great personal risk. Once two of them went to Hanworth in Middlesex because they had heard that a cock-fight was going to happen: together with two friends called in to act as strong-arm men and the then Secretary of the Society, they lay in wait in a pub called the *Swan* at Hanworth. Warned of their presence, the 'cockers' launched a savage attack: covered with blood, the Inspectors fought a retreating battle to another pub near by. Meanwhile the Secretary had managed to call for the help of six men from the Bow Street patrol. The police arrested the cock-fighters, though not before one of the Inspectors, James Piper, had been so badly beaten up that he died in hospital. Later his death was found to be due to tuberculosis, but clearly it had been accelerated by his

Mrs. Catherine Smithies, founder of the Band of Mercy.
Certificates of Merit, *below*, were given for acts of kindness to animals.

injuries. Partly as a consequence of the tragedy, it was decided that in future Inspectors should be issued with uniform, which would increase the public respect for them, or at least make potential attackers think again. As a still more practical measure, they were also issued with truncheons.

One effect of the Society's growing strength was the way it was able to encourage the spread of the animal welfare movement overseas. As early as 1834 a member of the committee, Sir John de Beauvoir, had been to Paris to advise on the starting of a French society. In Germany the first society for animal defence had begun at Stuttgart in 1837. Three years later came the founding of a separate SPCA for Scotland: though the Scottish Society has remained autonomous, relations continue to be most friendly. In 1859 the British Consul-General in the Netherlands was asked for copies of the English animal protection laws by the Dutch government, which wanted to adapt them. Two years later Belgium passed similar laws, this time as the result of an approach from the Society.

The United States had no cruelty laws till 1866. When they did come, it was largely as a result of the work of Henry Bergh, a former secretary of the American Legation in St. Petersburg. During his time in Russia, Bergh had been stirred by the suffering of animals there. Passing through London on his way back to the United States, he met John Colam, the Chief Secretary of the RSPCA. Bergh became fired with the idea of starting a similar society in New York. Within weeks of returning to America, he began work, and at a meeting in February 1866 the New York SPCA was formed.

One incident connected with its early days is worth the telling – if only to refute the charge that people concerned with animal welfare are less concerned with children. The story is told by A. W. Moss as follows:

One day, a lady who did charitable work in New York was sitting by the bedside of a dying woman when she asked: 'Is there anything more I can do for you?' and received the reply: 'You have done everything, but in the next room there lives a woman who has a child whom she leaves alone every morning without giving anything to eat, and when this woman comes home at night, she punishes the poor child so severely that her cries and shrieks distress me.'

The lady accepted the message as a dying charge and went to the police, who told her that that they could not interfere between parents and their children. She then consulted her lawyer. He tried to persuade her from pursuing the matter and refused to take up the

Band of Mercy magazine covers, 1907.
'We feed the Birds and make Dumb
Creatures Happy', ran the caption.
Below, 'Our Little Hero in the
Witness Box'.

case. Undaunted, the lady went to Mr. Bergh. She told him, 'There is a little animal suffering from the unkind treatment of a bad woman.' She won his sympathy and he promised to interfere on behalf of the 'little animal'! He was then told the victim in question was a child.

'Well, you have done this cleverly,' he replied, 'and I will not go back on my promise.' The S.P.C.A. investigated the matter and brought the case before the court. It was contended successfully that the child was an animal, Mr. Bergh was commended and the child was given proper care. Soon Mr. Bergh had so many cases of cruelty to children brought to him that a New York Society for the Prevention of Cruelty to Children was formed.

Within a year or so, Moss goes on, a similar organization was started in London, largely through John Colam and the RSPCA committee. At a meeting at the Mansion House in London, Lord Shaftesbury proposed the formation of a London Society for the Prevention of Cruelty to Children. The motion was seconded by Dr. Barnardo, and supported by Cardinal Manning. Later the RSPCA strengthened the link by offering the use of their own offices for meetings. Thus began a long and happy co-operation between the Society and the NSPCC which still continues.

*

One principle which has always been at the heart of the RSPCA's work is that of education. In its broadest sense it is what the Society is about – not only the prevention of cruelty, but the positive teaching of kindness.

Right from its earliest days, the Society had applied this idea of teaching in a literal sense. As early as 1845 it had begun to co-operate with the National Schools Society, which agreed that teachers should deal with kindness to animals in class, and that books on the subject should be placed in school libraries.

Soon the Society was distributing literature to workhouses and Ragged Schools. In 1860 the committee evidently thought it might be edifying for children to listen to the proceedings of the Society's annual general meeting, for it invited a thousand of them to attend it. There is no record of what the children thought, but they may have found the speeches worth it, for each child was given a penny bun. Another time we find the committee giving £10 to help a boy named James

Botheridge, who had given fearless evidence in a cruelty case, to remain at school. Such gestures may carry a hint of patronage today, but in Victorian times they must have seemed rare examples of the milk of human kindness.

Later in the century there would come the founding of a junior movement. The origin of the Band of Mercy, as it became known, was a children's branch founded at Wood Green by Mrs. Catherine Smithies, who was also a worker for the anti-slavery movement and a friend of both Lord Shaftesbury and of Harriet Beecher Stowe. Members of the Band promised to be kind to animals and birds and were issued with a badge and a monthly magazine entitled *Band of Mercy*. Apart from this, the main feature of membership seems to have been that favourite Victorian mode of instilling virtue, essay-writing: though competitions for the best essays were held throughout the country, much the largest was the annual London Competition, which in one year produced the daunting total of 40,000 essays. Prizes, sometimes a set of the complete works of Scott or Dickens, were distributed, usually at the Crystal Palace, to the accompaniment of hymns played on the organ.

*

Meanwhile how did the Society stand as it approached the completion of its first fifty years? By 1874, what had once seemed the impossible dream of an obscure East End clergyman had achieved the status of an institution. Its headquarters had now moved into the new premises in Jermyn Street which were to remain the Society's home for almost a hundred years. To those who could remember them, it must have seemed a far cry to the days when the founder had been imprisoned for debt.

The range and scope of the activities had also widened. Within ten years of its Jubilee the Society would be employing eighty Inspectors. Apart from its Royal Patron, distinguished men from all walks of life were associated with the RSPCA. Charles Dickens was a member, and in the Jubilee year Darwin, the naturalist, offered £50 to the Society for an invention which would humanely keep down rabbits. (Fifteen years earlier his *Origin of Species* had effectively demolished the theory of man as a superior creature, but its full effect was not yet felt. If anything, Darwin had done the animals a bad turn because of the increase in experiments on them, following the new interest in biology.)

105 Jermyn Street. The Headquarters of the RSPCA
from 1869 till 1973, when the Society moved to Horsham.

There had been no major legislation since Pease's Act of 1835 improving conditions in slaughter-houses, but in the 1860s a series of minor Acts were passed, mostly concerned with the protection of wild birds.

But such measures only chipped at the surface. It was true that some of the more outrageous horrors such as bull-baiting were ended for good, and that very slowly the Society was spreading patches of light in the cruelty that enfolded Victorian England like some impenetrable fog. The worst sufferers of all were the horses – the pit-ponies, the cab horses, and above all the decrepit horses that were exported to the continent for meat. Often, says A. W. Moss at pages 97–98 of *Valiant Crusade*:

> they were in such poor condition, so lame and diseased, that the Veterinary College at Brussels used to send its students to Antwerp to see the arrival of these British horses which were possessed of almost every conceivable ailment. . . . The horses were required to walk – crawl might be a better term – four and a half miles from the docks at Antwerp to the abattoirs. Whilst these ghastly processions were passing, many Belgians pulled down their blinds and closed their shutters as a protest against the iniquity.

The plight of the horses drawing London trams and buses was not much better. Working fifteen hours at a stretch, forced to be always starting and stopping amid the London traffic, and with no bar to the use of the driver's whip, it was not surprising that the London General Omnibus Company had to destroy a thousand maimed or exhausted horses every year. Cab horses, especially those used by drivers on the night-shift, would also be worked till they dropped dead. Because

Queen Victoria was a supporter of the Society in its early years.
In 1840 she gave it the prefix 'Royal'.

of the poor street lighting, their condition could not be seen even by those who might have been moved to protest.

Here and there the Society was able to alleviate such conditions. A fund was started to buy 'decayed and worn-out horses' and so stop their export. A special harness making conditions much easier for a horse drawing a two-wheeled cart, was imported from the United States on the recommendation of Henry Bergh, and brought into general use through the Society. Lectures on better horse care were given to what seem to have been surprisingly large gatherings of drivers, and in one year, 1881, fifty thousand copies of the Society's *Horse Book* were distributed. By 1895 a special staff of Inspectors was patrolling the roads leading to the East Coast ports from which the traffic to Belgium was carried on, with the result that in a few years there were literally thousands of convictions.

In 1911 came the most comprehensive piece of legislation so far. This was the Animals Protection Act, steered through the House of Commons by Sir George Greenwood, Liberal M.P. for Peterborough. Hailed as the 'Animals' Charter', it raised the maximum fine from £5 to £25, and the maximum term of imprisonment from three to six months. It covered almost every imaginable form of ill-treatment and is still, in the words of the legal handbook issued to Inspectors, the basis of the great majority of the Society's prosecutions.

Meanwhile the large-scale suffering of horses and donkeys continued well into this century. Now retired after a lifetime in the service of the Society, Chief Inspector Teddy Winn of Eastbourne told me how, as a young Inspector in the first World War, he used to stand watching the donkeys drawing loads of munitions over the cobbles at Woolwich Ferry.

In those days the roads were cobbles and flint, not sanded. When it rained they used to get greasy, so the horses and donkeys would slither about. The horses were rationed and they were overloaded; to make matters worse, there was the inexperience of young drivers. That was because of the war: what happened was that the boy at the back of the van took the reins, when the driver joined the army. If I saw one of them beating a donkey, I'd shout, then pull them in to the side, where I'd have a policeman handy. All the policemen in Deptford and Greenwich knew me. They used to call me the Donkey Huey, short for Humane . . . The magistrate at Deptford was an animal-lover. When he saw me, he used to leave the court and go round to the pound where the animals were kept – he'd get me to point out the unnecessary suffering.

HUMANE KILLERS

For Horses, Cattle, Pigs, Sheep, Calves, Dogs, and other Anima's.

1 & 1a. The R.S.P.C.A. LARGE HUMANE KILLER - - - Price £4 0s. 0d.

Cartridges, 13 - per 100.

NOTE The HUMANE KILLER is intended for killing large animals only, such as horses, bulls, oxen, heifers and large pigs, i.e., sows and boars, and should not be used for calves, sheep, ordinary pigs and smaller animals.

2. The R.S.P.C.A. SLAUGHTERING PISTOL - - - Price £3 5s. 0d.

Cartridges, '380 Revolver Smokeless, 10 - per 100.

For Horse Slaughterers. This is similar to the Large Humane Killer, but it is fitted with a short handle so that it can be used with one hand. To avoid confusion this instrument has been called the R.S.P.C.A. slaughtering pistol.

3. The "---" CAPTIVE BOLT PISTOL - - - Price £5 0s. 0d.

Cartridges, 3 6 per 100.

4 & 5. The GREENER "SAFETY" PISTOL - - - Price £2 10s. 0d.

Cartridges, 3 - and 2 - per 100. For use on Calves, Pigs, Sheep, Goats and Dogs.

6. The SWEDISH KILLER - - - - - Price (Sloped) £0 19s. 6d.

Cartridges, 11 - per 100. Strong (for Bulls) 2 - per dozen.

FOR USE ON ALL TYPES OF ANIMALS BY USING CARTRIDGES OF DIFFERENT STRENGTHS.

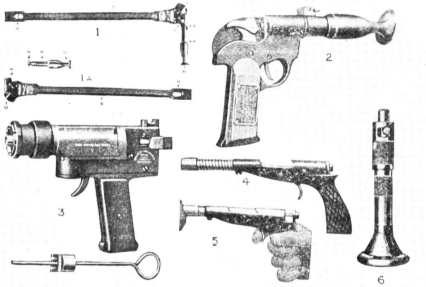

The above are supplied at cost price, Carriage Paid, by

The R.S.P.C.A., 105 JERMYN ST., LONDON, S.W.1.

Humane killers and pistols. The RSPCA cattle killer, produced in 1907, marked the beginning of humane slaughtering methods.

Sometimes the inexperience of the drivers was to blame, sometimes it was downright cruelty. They used to have a steel-lined whip with the end bent, so it'd cut into the horse like a fish-hook. You'd get mouth-soreness from the bits tugging, and you'd get cases of over-driving, sores, or lameness. And a lot of those animals were suffering from malnutrition . . .

In the end the suffering only finished with the end of horse-drawn traffic. I always say when Mr. Morris gave us the motor-car, he did a good turn to the horses.

Many other such examples could be quoted. But now, as we begin to approach our own time, we must hurry the story on, for this look into the past is intended not as a detailed history but as a background to the present.

In 1924 the Society celebrated its centenary. The occasion was marked by an Ode by Thomas Hardy, not, it must be said, in his most lyric vein, and by the publication of the first history of the RSPCA, *A Century of Work for Animals* by E. G. Fairholme and Wellesley Pain. Fairholme was the Chief Secretary of the Society, and it is worth noting some of the problems and achievements dealt with in the book's closing chapters. Among the recent achievements it recorded was the abolition of the black plumes worn by horses at funerals. 'A plume weighed about 6 lbs, and in wet and windy weather the wearing of these plumes caused discomfort and in many cases actual suffering to the horses.' The Society's view had been put to the Undertakers' Association, and the practice discontinued.

Meanwhile there were other problems besides funeral plumes to worry about. The worn-out horse trade to the continent still continued, despite the efforts of Lord Lambourne, Chairman of the Society, who introduced a Bill in the Lords to try to stop it. Pit-ponies were another cause of concern, though Fairholme and Pain were able to note a slow improvement in conditions. Among other things deplored was the plight of circus animals, and the practice of slaughtering herons for their feathers, to be used in the making of ladies' hats.

Such were the problems the Society faced in 1924. Meanwhile, in its centenary year, it could look back on a solid measure of achievement. It had largely inspired the 1911 Act, which in range and authority far exceeded the animal protection laws of any country. It had attained a unique public recognition and esteem, and laid down the basic guidelines with which it would operate in the future – the Inspectors, the branches, the promotion of legislation, and the first stages in educating a new generation in animal welfare.

32

A continuing problem in the early 1900s was the export of worn-out horses to the continent for sale as horsemeat.

Punch's comment on the worn-out horse trade, in a cartoon by Bernard Partridge. 'Have you anything to declare?' asks the Customs officer at Antwerp. 'Only this', says the horse, 'that I'm ashamed of my country.'

Younger and older animal lovers on television. Retired Chief Inspector Teddy Winn (*below*) was featured in *This Is Your Life* with Eamonn Andrews.

What had been achieved, in fact, was the basis of the modern Society – the Society which, over the next fifty years, would find itself facing problems of animal exploitation on a scale undreamt-of in the 1920s.

Later we shall look at these problems in some detail. But what we must turn to next is the Society, as it is now. We begin, as Arthur Broome began, with the Inspectors.

Royal Society
for the Prevention of Cruelty to Animals,
105 JERMYN STREET, LONDON, S.W.

RETURN of CONVICTIONS for the month of SEPTEMBER, 1909.

HORSES	Beating, kicking, stoning, etc.	35
„	Compelling to search for food with injured limbs	1
„	Overdriving	5
„	Overloading	13
„	Starving by withholding food	1
„	Travelling decrepit horses (1,537 were exported during the month)	
„	Travelling (unharnessed) when lame	8
„	Working in an unfit state	5
„	Wounding by violently spurring at races	275
DONKEYS	Beating, kicking, stoning, etc.	9
„	Working in an unfit state	6
„	Wounding by hoppling improperly	1
„	Wounding by inserting stick into private parts	1
CATTLE	Beating, kicking, stoning, etc.	1
„	Overstocking	1
„	Starving by withholding food	1
SHEEP	Beating, kicking, stoning, etc.	1
GOATS	Working in an unfit state	1
„	Wounding by hoppling improperly	1
DOGS	Beating, kicking, stoning, etc.	7
„	Killing improperly with consequent suffering	1
„	Suffocating in box during transit by rail	1
„	Wounding by throwing into the sea	1
„	Wounding by dashing on ground	2
CATS	Abandoning down disused well	1
„	Beating, kicking, stoning, etc.	12
„	Starving by withholding food	2
„	Wounding by docking tail	1
„	Wounding by setting dogs to worry	1
„	Wounding by shooting when trespassing	1
RABBITS	Starving by withholding food	1
FOWLS	Conveying improperly in sacks	6
„	Overcrowding in crates	2
„	Overcrowding in boxes	1
„	Starving by withholding food	1
„	Wounding by tying legs too tightly	2
DUCKS	Conveying improperly in sacks	1
LINNETS	Starving by withholding food	2
„	Wounding with braces as "decoys"	1
WILD BIRDS	Offences during close season	5
VARIOUS	Assaulting Inspector	1
„	Causing in above (owners)	153
		577
	Total during 1909 up to last return	4,434
	Total for the present year commencing January 1st, 1909	5,011

34 offenders were committed to Prison; 543 offenders paid pecuniary penalties; 24 persons were acquitted, but the Society's costs were remitted, which justifies the Society's action; 99 persons guilty of minor acts of cruelty were admonished in writing.

The Council invite the co-operation and support of the public. Besides day-duty, relays of Inspectors watch all-night traffic in the streets of London.

The names of Complainants are not given up when letters are marked "private."

E. G. FAIRHOLME, Secretary.

Convictions in September 1909. Far the greatest number were for cruelty to horses.

2 : The Inspector's World

> 'An Inspector combines widely different callings. At times a lawyer, a veterinary surgeon, and an organiser, he is also called upon for advice on many different subjects and receives the confidences of many people. Like Agag, he must walk delicately, and his conduct must be above suspicion.' – *RSPCA Inspectors' Legal Handbook.*

A Cow Called Lucky

'Can you tell me where Rigg Hall Farm is? I'm looking for the RSPCA man.'

'Ay. He's up there yonder.' The tractor driver pointed the way on from the farm track I had come up. It was marked, accurately, unsuitable for motors. 'You need to follow t'stone wall round to the right. Then drive on the grass where you see t'car tracks.'

I thanked the tractor driver and drove on. In the early morning sea-fret you couldn't see much – stone walls, green fields, a couple of remote hill farms on the skyline. A little way back on the road was the village of Stainton Dale, a few miles north of Scarborough.

It had been late the previous evening that I had had a phone call from Inspector Maynard of the RSPCA. Three heifers had gone over a 500-foot cliff face and landed in some undergrowth. One was dead and another was in a bad way. With luck, Inspector Maynard said, there was a chance of saving the third one. He himself had spent all day in the undergrowth, trying to set up a system of pulleys which would haul the heifer to the cliff top: working with a team of local coastguards, he had got the rescue arrangements set up on the previous evening. Today, if everything went all right, he hoped to get at least one heifer up the cliff.

So now, if I was not too late, I was going to see a rescue. I drove on past more stone walls, then came to a gate where there were car tracks on the grass. A few hundred yards further on, there was a collection of vans and tractors on the cliff top. Just before I reached them, I saw, for the first time, the cliff face.

It was far steeper than the Inspector's description, almost completely sheer. Somewhere near the foot it curved slightly. Beyond the curve, and far below me, was a wild terrain of trees and scrub. Beyond that, in turn, was the sea, or what you could see of it. From this height it had the stillness it has from the air, a fringe of surf like a lace tablecloth. Everything else was hidden in mist.

If I had wanted to see a dramatic setting for a rescue, this was it. I stopped the car on the grass, and was greeted by a shortish, friendly looking man who was putting on a canvas jacket.

'You made it then? I'm Inspector Maynard.' He wasn't obviously tough-looking, but there was a springiness and wiriness about him like a sprig of heather. 'You're just in time to see us go down.'

'Us?'

'Mr. Wilson's the vet from Scarborough. He's going down with me to sedate the heifers. We're hoping to bring one up this morning.'

'What about the other?'

'We'll see what shape she's in when we get down there.' He led the way to the cliff edge; it was smooth and muddy where the ropes had worn it. Far below us the sea-fret still rolled in swathes over the scrub. 'That's where they are, down there in that thicket. The one that's all right is pretty lively. That's why she's got to be sedated before we can bring her up.'

'How did they come to get down there?' It seemed incredible that any living creature could have gone over such a height, and survived.

'It was a bit of bad luck. They'd all three been let in this field for the first time yesterday morning.' Inspector Maynard looked round at the rich, lush grass, soaked by the rain of the North Riding. 'When they saw the grass they must have got over-excited. They started playing and pushing each other by the wall, and next thing they'd all gone over. Fortunately there was enough scrub to break their fall, except for the one that died. She was killed when she hit the bottom.'

'How are you going to get the others up?'

'We're making a sort of aerial railway.' He pointed to the edge of the next field, where there was a Land-Rover marked 'HM Coastguards' and a string of helpers. 'The coastguards have brought a tripod and pulleys. We're going to set the tripod down below, put the beast in a net, then try and haul her up, wide of the cliff face.'

I looked down again at the scrub below. 'Isn't it going to be very difficult to swing her clear?' Between the cliff face and rope, it seemed, there would never be enough angle to avoid the bushes and twisted trees that sprouted from the cliff.

'We've a crane coming at half-past one. That'll project clear of the cliff, then swing her round to about here, where we're standing.' He broke off to say good morning to a large, amiable-looking man with spectacles, whose few wisps of hair were flying about in the wind like pennants. 'This is Mr. Arnold Wilson, the vet from Scarborough.'

Mr Wilson greeted me, adjusting the ropes round his middle. Then he went over to his car and got several bottles of drugs and syringes which he put in a big pink plastic bag.

'What are you going to do when you get down there?'

'I'm worried about the cow that's injured. I don't think she's going to make it. We'll have a look at her first, then sedate the other one.'

By now the preparations on the cliff top were almost complete. Mr. Wilson and the Inspector prepared for their descent, ropes tied round their waists in thick coils. In charge of the cliff-top party lowering them down was a bluff-looking Whitby coastguard with a cheerful line in nautical humour.

'Haul her away, lads! Heave away! Are you all right, Arnold?'

Mr. Wilson kept his hands rather precariously on the rope as if he was riding a bicycle, and grinned. 'I'd feel a lot happier in my surgery.'

One of the other coastguards peered down over the edge. 'It's a job for a bloody steeplejack down there.'

'Don't look at the cliff face, look at me', called the Chief Coastguard encouragingly. 'Look at me, Arnold. I'm a good-looking fellow.' The mixture of farm hands, holiday makers and teenagers on the ropes all laughed. All the same, you could feel the tension.

Soon both men were down, hand-over-hand on the rope with their feet catching at footholds. Far below the mist lifted slightly. In the haze, we glimpsed a patch of black and white.

'That's one of the beasts down there. They're both Friesians.' The Chief Coastguard turned, getting ready his impedimenta of blocks, pulleys, and the tripod that was to be sent down next. Meanwhile the radio in the Land-Rover had begun to crackle. One of the other coast-guards was already down there, sending messages to the party on the cliff top.

'Mr. Wilson and the Inspector are down. They're having a look at the injured beast.' There was a long pause in the activity, while more pulleys were got ready. After a bit there was another crackle and the coastguard's voice came back. 'They've decided to dispose of her', he said, as if he hoped the words might blur the meaning.

We heard a shot far down in the scrub, then silence. It didn't seem a very good start to the day, but it was early yet. Overhead the sun was beginning to come through, its June heat beginning to burn up the sea-fret.

*

A rescue may sound dramatic, but in the event few things could be more slow-moving. Over the next three hours we watched while various bits of equipment were laboriously sent down – the tripod, the blocks and pulleys, a huge pink net, big as a herring trawl, for the heifer to be brought up in. Every so often something would seem to be happening, then a rope would get caught on a tree or a bit of scrub, and there would be a fresh delay.

'We want you to pull that rope up.'

'Which one?' Even by one o'clock the Chief Coastguard sounded good-humoured. 'We've got six bloody ropes up here.' Presently the farmer's wife came and brought sandwiches and cups of strong tea with sugar. A patriarchal-looking farmer came from a neighbouring farm. He had got a case of milk fever among his cows, and wanted to know when Mr. Wilson would be finished.

'Looks as if he might be there till five o'clock', said somebody, and the farmer who had come for help decided to stop and give a hand on the ropes, and I suddenly thought of the Old Testament law about helping your brother if his ox or ass fell by the wayside.

By now everyone was pulling. The vet and Inspector Maynard had got the heifer in the net, and wanted her raised a little. Meanwhile up on the cliff there was a sudden shout from someone. Over the whaleback curve, a huge yellow object was advancing.

'It's the crane!'

It chugged on, and came to rest within feet of the edge. A lean, tanned man got out, looked over the scene with the coastguard, then began driving great shafts in the ground to secure it. Slowly, the great yellow arm nosed out, clear of the cliff top.

Now everything depended on the securing of the net. Far below we could see tiny figures moving perilously between the bits of scrub on the cliff face. The whine of the crane stopped for a moment, and we could hear Inspector Maynard's voice on the radio, sounding urgent.

'This beast's going to die if we don't get her up quickly.'

We did not know it at the time, but afterwards Inspector Maynard told me there had been a moment when the heifer had actually stopped breathing. When a cow is anaesthetized, he explained, a pressure of natural digestive gas builds up and presses on the diaphragm. Mr. Wilson had had to put his hand inside her mouth to pull her tongue farther out, to let this gas escape.

39

Of this we on the cliff top knew nothing. All we could do now was watch while the great yellow crane arm pushed out farther. The hook began to go down slowly on its brown hawser.

'If only they can keep it clear of the branches.' The cheerful coastguard peered down. Now you could hear the slow click-click of the crane's pulley. Hundreds of feet of the hawser must have gone down, but there was still more coming. There came another interminable pause, then the radio crackled again.

'We've got her secure! Haul her up!'

Slowly the hawser began to coil back. We could see the great weight of the net draw clear of the scrub.

'This is the bit where you keep your fingers crossed.' I looked round. It was Mr. Wilson, who had just hauled himself up, his face covered in chalk and scratches.

'Is she going to be all right?'

'As long as we can keep the net clear of those bushes. If it touches, and the net begins to spin, she's done for. It all depends on her keeping the same position.'

The whine of the winch went on – then suddenly, far quicker than anyone had expected, we saw the great shape of the net appearing over the cliff edge. It swung to the right, and even over the scream of the winch you could hear a gasp of delight. Sticking out from the padded folds of the net was something recognizably cow-like, a white creamy-looking muzzle. Next moment the net was being gently lowered to the cliff side, and Mr. Wilson was deftly cutting the strings. For an agonizing moment he knelt down, listening to the heifer's pulse and heart-beat.

'She's all right.'

Nearly forty people had been engaged in the rescue for five hours and forty minutes. For them, three words of Mr. Wilson's had made it all seem worth it.

*

Ten minutes later I stood with Inspector Maynard. Scratched, muddy, and cheerful, he had just come over the cliff face.

'I had to make sure she was all right.'

He went over and patted the heifer, then came back munching a sandwich.

In the end, I asked, does saving an animal's life really justify so much risk? Inspector Maynard took a swig of hot strong tea and nodded. 'All those beasts were insured, so there'd have been no loss to the farmer. Only when it comes down to it, you think there's something alive down there. You can't leave it to die, any more than you would a person.'

Everyone was glowing with the warm feeling of an experience shared. People who had never met before today were arranging to go home for tea with each other, young and old alike were re-living the tense moments on the cliff top. The Inspector went over to have another look at the heifer, and Mr. Wilson came and stood beside me.

'What really took guts was what Geoff Maynard did yesterday. He went down alone on that rope when nobody else was here. I'm going to write to the RSPCA about him.'

Only one living creature on the whole cliff top was taking it all casually, and that was the little heifer. Out to the world, she lay on her side, her head propped on the folds of the net that had brought her to safety.

One of the local reporters wanted to know if she had a name. The farmer's wife said no, she hadn't – could anyone think of one? After all the animal had been through, it was agreed, she ought to have one.

The cheerful coastguard grinned. 'I think it should be Lucky.'

Inspector at Work

Inspector Geoff Maynard is one of 200 RSPCA Inspectors throughout the country. If the heart of the Society can be said to be the branches, then the Inspectors are its hands. Essentially the Inspector is the man who carries out the claim implicit in the Society's title – he prevents cruelty to animals.

It is by no means his only task. In the course of his career he will, as we have just seen, be called on to rescue animals from every kind of natural hazard. He will have to deal with animals maddened and made dangerous by human cruelty. When nobody else knows what to do with an animal, it is the RSPCA Inspector they send for.

The 200 Inspectors are spread over the whole area of England and Wales; Scotland and Northern Ireland have their own separate organizations. An area may be a large town, or several hundred square miles in a rural district. Within his area or 'patch' as he usually calls it, an Inspector will have to know everything that can affect animal welfare within it, ranging from cattle markets to pet shops and riding schools. He is usually on first-name terms with the police and the local fire-service, and well known as a local figure. Animal stories being as popular with newspaper readers as they are, the RSPCA man is likely to get more column-inches in the local paper than anyone else except the Mayor.

The Inspector's map. The coloured sections represent
areas covered by each of the Society's 200 Inspectors. Scotland
and Northern Ireland have their own societies.

When an Inspector has been some years in the service he may be promoted to Chief Inspector. Roughly one in four Inspectors become a Chief, and roughly one in four Chiefs become a Travelling Superintendent. The Travellers, as they are known, have responsibility for the regions. Another five Superintendents are based at the Society's head-quarters at Horsham, where apart from training new Inspectors, their most important job is to prepare prosecutions. Apart from these there is one full-time Docks Inspector, and forty-one part-time Inspectors, often retired policemen, who cover markets.

What is a working day like for the average Inspector in the field? Usually it is a ten-hour one, possibly with odd breaks for cups of coffee but no specific lunch hour. When he does get home he is still on call,

The Inspector's daily round. If a dog is injured in a road accident, it will be the RSPCA man who is sent for.

with a strong probability of having to go out at night, or perhaps at six o'clock in the morning to put down a dog injured in a road accident. In theory an Inspector gets alternate weekends off, but unless he goes right away, even this is likely to be interrupted. 'You eat, sleep, drink it', said one Inspector based on a rural district. 'Even on your weekend off, people will come round with some animal in trouble. You can't let 'em down.'

More than most people's lives, the Inspector's is built round the telephone. Between 8.30 and 9.30 in the morning there will be a series of calls which will form the basis of his day's work. When he comes back at around six o'clock in the evening, there will be a further clutch of calls from people who have been uncertain about phoning earlier. 'You get a woman living on an estate', said one urban Inspector, 'who's been bothered all day about a neighbour's dog being shut up. She doesn't want to stick her neck out and make trouble – so she waits until her husband comes home and lets him decide.' The proliferation of morning and evening calls does not mean that the phone is idle in the day. I went round with one Inspector for four hours and when we got back he asked his wife if there had been any calls. 'Thirty-two', she said. Neither of them seemed to think it was in any way unusual. In the nature of the job, the Inspector's wife has to be as sympathetic, helpful, and almost as knowledgeable as he is.

The average Inspector spends more than half his time in the small blue Escort van which is the Society's standard issue. The van has a radio link with the Securicor network so that the Inspector can send or receive urgent messages: in it he also carries the tools of his trade. Apart from such relatively obvious items as drugs, ropes, overalls, and a humane killer, the list includes an instrument called a grasper, which is a long metal rod with a collar that can be used to capture a dangerous dog. There is a swan crook, which does what its name implies and can be very useful, as one Inspector said, if you're being hissed at by an angry swan. There are extending rods rather like those used by plumbers. These can be attached to the grasper and used to rescue an injured bird at a height of more than thirty feet.

Strictly speaking, an RSPCA Inspector's actual powers are no more than those of any other citizen. With his dark blue uniform, peaked cap and light blue shirt, he may look like a policeman and is often taken for one. In fact he has no right of entry and cannot actually charge anyone with cruelty.

But in any case of animal cruelty it is the RSPCA man the police will look to. His knowledge of the laws protecting animals is deeper than theirs, and it is his speciality. In this sense, the modern Inspector is

Kid-glove treatment for two baby owls.

the direct descendant of Arthur Broome's Inspector Wheeler. The difference, of course, is that in Wheeler's time there was only one law. In the legal guide which all Inspectors carry today, there are more than forty listed.

When legal action does need to be taken, the Inspector will first supply the details to the Society's headquarters. Here the reports will be studied by three specially trained Superintendents, working in the Society's Legal Department. If they decide the case is one which should be brought to court, they will instruct the Inspector on the spot to 'lay information' with the local Magistrate's Clerk, who will then issue a summons. When the case does come to court, it will normally be the Inspector's evidence on which the Prosecution's case will rest.

What happens when an Inspector actually has to caution someone or to start a prosecution? One man who has as much experience of

In the course of his work the Inspector
co-operates with many other people.

prosecutions as anyone is Ronald Butfield, the Society's energetic and
highly articulate Chief Superintendent. What does an Inspector
actually feel, I asked him, when he comes across a case of cruelty?

'I think any Inspector worth his salt develops a sort of in-built anger.
I'm not talking about an animal that's being beaten. I'm talking about
some friendly old dog that's being kept in a tatty old box for a kennel,
perhaps left out in the hot sun with a great thick collar that chafes its
neck. Suppose that dog is handed over, and you take him home and get
to know him. Once he realizes you're not going to belt him, he can't
give you enough affection. In a case like that I'd feel what I call this
in-built anger. I'd take the greatest pleasure in going back to the owner
and telling him in very accurate legal terms what I proposed doing if I
found him ill-treating a dog again.'

'What about a case where you're actually going to prosecute?'

'A prosecution's very different. If I'm giving a caution I might say a few things that aren't in the rule book, but if there's a precaution pending, then it's out of my hands.' One of the worst cases he had ever had, said Mr. Butfield, was of a man who had buried his Alsatian: one evening between teatime and supper, he had decided he didn't want it. 'He smashed it on the head with a coal-hammer and left it in the yard to die. After a while his kids came in and said it was making funny noises. The man was indoors watching the telly – I remember the thing that shocked me most was that he could remember the name of the programme he was watching. So he went out and smashed its head again six times with a garden spade. This time he succeeded in chopping its ears off and part of its nostrils. Then he buried it. The post-mortem showed it had been buried alive – it had died in its own blood, of asphyxiation.'

'What did you feel when you went round to see him?'

'I just felt this cold super-efficient anger. I'd have made a shocking NSPCC Inspector, because I'd never have been able to keep my hands to myself. What happens with cruelty to animals is that I just go terribly cold. My brain begins to click beautifully. Everything slots into place.'

Had he sometimes, I asked, felt sorry for someone when there was going to be a prosecution? Mr. Butfield said that he often did in court, especially if there were some extenuating circumstances. 'Or if, when you see them, you realize they're truly sorry. Then it just seems terrible that they couldn't have shown this humanity before. Sometimes you get some odd cases. One I always remember was when I was an Inspector in the Cheltenham area. There was a chap I knew had a pony and cart – we'll call him Tommy Jones. One day Tommy'd been out drinking and he put his pony at a gallop up Birdlip Hill. Somebody had said it was cruel and there'd been a fight outside the pub. The local policeman had rung me – when I got there the pony was still sweating, the water running off and lying in puddles. So the police got the usual statement of suffering from the vet, and they charged Tommy with various offences, including cruelty. What niggled me was that I wasn't sure it *was* cruelty. That pony was grass-fed, and a grass-fed pony'll always sweat. The other thing is that it's kinder to let a horse take a hill at a gallop, if it's got a cart behind it. It's much better than making it sweat up slowly, step by step.'

'So what happened in the end?'

'In the end Tommy got three months on the other charges, and the option of an extra month or a £20 fine for cruelty. When the magistrate asked him what he was going to do, he said he'd like a word with me. I couldn't imagine what he was going to ask, but he explained the position quickly. He'd got £20 in his pocket, and he could have paid the fine. But meanwhile he was going to prison for three months anyway, and he was worried about who was going to feed his horses. He said if he didn't pay the fine and gave me the £20 to buy food, would I feed them? So I said I would, and then he went back in the dock and told the magistrate he'd go to prison. By giving me the £20 to feed the horses, he'd got himself another month inside.'

How much, I asked, had the ways of cruelty changed – was there still as much of what one could call ignorant cruelty as there used to be? Mr. Butfield considered the question thoughtfully and said that on the whole there wasn't. 'You'll still get the occasional pathological case, and you'll still get the kind of cruelty that comes from people who I suppose must be mentally subnormal. I think the biggest change is that the type of ignorance is different. You'll get someone who buys an animal as a sort of status symbol. Perhaps they've seen the Alsatians on *Softly, Softly*, and they decide to buy one. What they don't realize is that an Alsatian's a high-powered dog, that needs a lot of exercise and training. Or perhaps someone thinks they'd like to buy a horse, without knowing how much grass it needs for pasture. Sometimes the animal-lovers can be the worst – I saw a lady myself in Horsham High Street this morning, carrying a little fat dachshund. I wanted to say to her, "Madam, why don't you do that dog a favour and let it walk?"'

How often does an Inspector have to deal with cases which may be followed by a caution or a prosecution? In an average month, Mr. Butfield told me, an Inspector might have one prosecution and up to twenty cautions.

Meanwhile the everyday part of the Inspector's world is what Mr. Butfield calls advice. 'Advice can be stopping a boy with an airgun to ask him what he proposes shooting with it, and whether he knows anything about the laws protecting wild birds. It can be a friendly word to somebody in a market who's not bothering too much how he loads his cattle.' Even though it is now no part of his official duties, Mr. Butfield told me, he never goes past a box of chicks at a railway station without having a look to see that they are properly packed and being well looked after.

'Being out of uniform doesn't break the habit?'

Mr. Butfield grinned and said it was only a matter of sticking your neck out a bit further. Only the previous week, he said, he had been at the seaside and watched a family trying to get their dog into the sea,

He must be as good at making contacts with humans –

– as well as animals.

although it was clearly frightened. 'Plain clothes have nothing to do with a dog being dropped into the sea when it doesn't want to go. On that particular occasion the chap told me to mind my bloody business. I happened to have my official card with me, so I had the pleasure of telling him it *was* my bloody business. On duty or not, if an Inspector sees a suffering animal, it's his duty to do something for it. If an Inspector hasn't got that inside him, he's no good to us.'

*

There is one aspect of the job which no Inspector likes, and that is having to put animals down. Few Inspectors will go through a week without having to destroy some animal – it may be anything from an unwanted litter of kittens to some hill-farmer's sheepdog. If the animal is clearly incurably ill, vicious or very old, the Inspector will painlessly destroy it without question.

But there are many cases where the issue is less clear-cut. 'What do you do', asked one Inspector, 'with the kind of people who bring round a perfectly healthy dog and ask you to put it down because they're going on holiday and don't want to pay for him going to kennels? Then they come back a month later, smiles all over their faces, saying they want another from the dogs' home.'

One local branch secretary told me of a woman who had re-decorated her house, and wanted the cat put down because it didn't match the new colours. Such cases may be extreme, but there are many others where the Inspector himself is called on to make a difficult decision. 'Once a family thinks it no longer wants its pet,' explained one Inspector, 'that family is unlikely to provide a good home. On the other hand, at least part of our job is to educate people to have a sense of responsibility about their pets.'

I went with one Midlands Inspector to see a family who had two seven-year-old poodles they thought they wanted put down. The problem was that now they had a small baby. The poodles had been a bit over-indulged in the past, had become jealous of the baby, and one of them had given somebody a nip. Now the parents were anxious because the baby was getting to an age where he might push the dogs around a bit, and they feared he might get bitten.

So what was this particular family going to do? They had been to the vet, who had refused to put down two healthy animals. They had tried the kennels where the poodles came from. The woman at the kennels had said she would try to find homes, but hadn't been hopeful.

Some animals are more appreciative than others!

Office work at the end of the day. Inspectors spend many hours writing reports, or preparing evidence for court cases.

When the Inspector and I arrived we found the owners distressed at the thought of having the dogs put down, worried about the baby, but above all anxious for the Inspector to make the decision. The poodles themselves were a couple of bouncy, cheerful-looking little dogs, a sort of smoky grey colour, with the kind of tawny tinge that poodles often have round their beards, as if they'd been at the orangeade. The Inspector looked them over and played with them a bit. After a while he told the owners he would put them down if that was what they wanted.

'If you really think it's best.'

'I think it's best because you do.' The Inspector spoke gently but with quiet authority – he wasn't letting them get away with putting the decision on to him. He asked the man if he would hold the dogs while he injected them, or even help him bury them, but the owner wouldn't. He didn't think he could bear to see his own dogs put down, he said, and the garden wasn't big enough to bury them.

54

Later I watched while the Inspector put the dogs down, swiftly, painlessly, and saying the kind of soft ridiculous things people do say to any animal in need of comfort. I asked him if he ever got used to it, and he said no. 'It's the worst thing we have to do. All Inspectors hate it. However many times we do it.'

Had he had doubts about putting the poodles down? 'On balance they'd decided they didn't want the dogs. Having come to that point, I realized it would be very difficult to find another home for them – they were too pampered, too temperamental. It isn't easy to place one dog, let alone two, at seven years old.'

All the same, he said he didn't blame the couple for wanting their dogs put down, because they were worried about the baby. 'What I do wish they could have done was to stay with them, or even help me bury them. That's where responsibility comes in. They didn't have it.'

Inspector Heritage of Aberystwyth found these gin-traps in a disused mine-shaft. Though gin-traps have been illegal in Britain since 1958, the export trade in them continues.

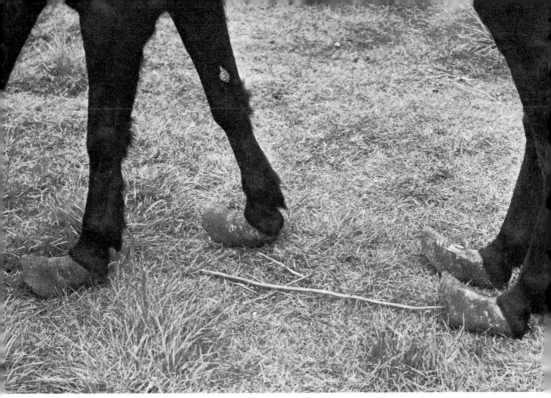

Cruelty through neglect. This horse's hooves had been
allowed to grow so long that it could hardly walk.

*

Apart from four-legged animals, an Inspector has to be able to deal
tactfully with everyone, from anxious old ladies and children worried
about lost pets, to farmers who may very likely resent inquiries into the
way they run their business. Often he has to be a kind of unofficial
social worker, for a family which is cruel to animals is often one where
children are neglected.

In his work for suffering animals, no Inspector can forget what
animals themselves can do for suffering or lonely people. Chief
Inspector John Ambrose's most treasured memory is of a boy called
Kevin. As the local Inspector at Oxford, Ambrose one day got a call
from the Nuffield Orthopaedic Centre. Could he come round to rescue
a canary which had flown into a ward where there were several polio
patients?

Ambrose went round, saw the canary flying about and thought it wouldn't be much of a problem to catch it. The sister in charge of the ward said that he might not have problems, but that she had. What had happened was that the bird had settled near where ten-year-old Kevin, over for treatment from Ireland, was lying in an iron lung. Kevin had made friends with the canary, and now wanted to know if he could keep it.

The hospital rules, it seemed, could be stretched if the canary could be found an adequate cage. Ambrose rang RSPCA Headquarters in London and asked what could be done. Within hours the finest canary-cage the Society could find was on its way to Oxford.

Inspector Ambrose's next problem was when the canary's original owner turned up. 'I told him we'd give him twenty canaries if he'd let us have this one', says Ambrose. 'Of course, as soon as he heard about

Cruelty through brutality. This donkey had been ridden round a field by a gang of boys. Left with a lacerated back, one broken foreleg, and an eye gouged out, it still nuzzled Mike Chester, Manager of the Mayhew Animal Home.

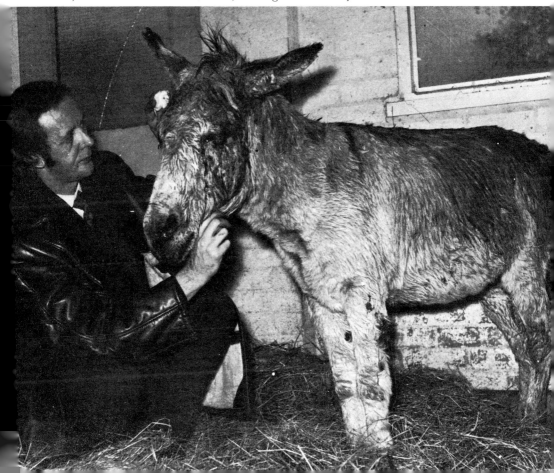

Kevin, there was no difficulty.' The canary was duly installed in its cage by Kevin's iron lung and christened Barry. For the next few weeks a visit to see both of them was on Inspector Ambrose's lists of regular calls.

A few weeks later Inspector Ambrose got a phone call – and was surprised when the voice at the other end was Kevin's. In a wheelchair now, he had propelled himself to the phone to ask if Ambrose could help once more. Now that he was better he was going home – but if Barry was to go too, the airline insisted it must be in a special travelling cage. Once again, Headquarters was able to produce what was needed. Writing to report their safe return a few weeks later, Kevin's mother thanked Inspector Ambrose. Nothing in the long weeks of suffering, she said, had meant as much to Kevin as the companionship of one small canary.

Apart from his qualities of humanity and understanding, an Inspector also needs to be tough. One man told me that in the space of two years he had been attacked with a sledgehammer and a hatchet. Superintendent Grinnall of the Headquarters staff showed me where he had been bitten by a dog thrown at him by the owner: the case had been one of thirty-five dogs being kept in a single room, so underfed that they had begun to eat each other. (Not all assaults are physical – one Inspector, investigating a case where a cat was alleged to have been sacrificed as part of a black magic ritual, received an effigy of himself with pins stuck in it.) Often an Inspector will find himself in households where he needs not only strong nerves but a strong nose. He has got to be tough enough to tackle a horse-dealer coming out of the beer tent at a pony sale, and gentle enough to care for an injured wren.

For all this, it must be said, the earnings are scarcely lavish. An Inspector's starting salary is £1100 a year, which will rise to just on £1700 if he reaches the rank of Chief Inspector. (It is true that he gets a free house and the use of his van for family purposes, but not every Inspector wants to take his children out at the weekend in a van which may habitually be used, among other things, for transporting dead cats.) Few Inspectors complain about the pay. Most, after all, have come in because the job is a rewarding one in other ways, and they like the independence. What does go against the grain is the lack of leisure, especially at a time when most other people are getting more. 'It's not the money', said one Inspector with a young family, 'it's the disproportion between me and my friends and neighbours, of not being able to get away from the job.'

One of the most trying hazards of an Inspector's life is the sort of

The Inspector's training school at Horsham.
Trainees listen to a lecture on animal protection laws,
and learn how to handle animals.

criticism which may be well-intentioned but not so well-informed. One particularly dedicated Inspector told me he had been the subject of two or three critical letters in the local press because he hadn't immediately gone to rescue a cat which had got itself up a tree. 'I happened to know that particular cat, and I knew it had been up and down that same tree by itself three times.' In the end the letters to the local press had come down on his side – all the same, he said, the criticism had hurt.

Another time I was with a younger Inspector, John Hutchinson of Chatham, visiting a lady whose life had been dedicated to cats: if there was one subject that really upset her, she said, it was the thought of cats being made to suffer.

Inspector Hutchinson happens to be very much involved with welfare work for children. Since the troubles in Northern Ireland, he has helped bring over mixed parties of Catholic and Protestant children for holidays in England. 'There's a lot of children suffering in the world, come to that', he said mildly.

Trainee Inspectors at the end of the six-month course.
With them, Major Ronald Seager, Executive Director of the Society.

Inspector afloat. One Lancashire Inspector started
this island sanctuary to protect lake birds attacked by vandals.

'Children? I suppose so.' All the same, she had almost visibly
switched off. Afterwards I asked him if he didn't find himself sometimes getting a bit irritable with the clients, and he grinned.

'That's the problem. In this job you can't get irritable and you can't
get too emotional. You just have to learn to sort 'em out in a nice
way.'

Being able to sort them out in a nice way does not quite complete the
list of attributes required. The Inspector must have the kind of
intuition and flair which comes from really caring about animals. One
Travelling Superintendent told me how once, on market duty in
Wiltshire, he had noticed that the cattle were terrified of rails or pens
that were painted black. When the railings were painted green, on
the other hand, they allowed themselves to be driven through easily.

The Superintendent had gone to the market authorities and
suggested they painted all the railings green. 'They were quite nice
about it, but made it clear they thought I was mildly potty. I kept on

about it, and in the end they did paint them green, I think just to humour me. In that market today there isn't a single black railing, and the cattle go through without any fear or trouble.'

*

Anyone who thinks animal-lovers are sentimental should meet Inspector John Kenny, whose patch is London's East End. Short, stocky, and red-bearded, Kenny is an ex-paratrooper and looks it. After he left the army he worked on newspapers for a while, then started a kennels in Shropshire. One day an RSPCA Inspector brought him a dog that had been ill-treated. Kenny built it up and decided, one can't help feeling a little to his own surprise, that from then on animal welfare was to be his vocation.

What, I asked him, were the particular problems in the East End? One of the main ones, he said, was Club Row, the street market for pets and birds, which often includes finches and linnets illegally trapped in Epping Forest. Only that morning he had spent a couple of hours at Epping police court, giving evidence against a man who had been caught trapping greenfinches. The man had been fined £2 on each of twenty-four birds, which Kenny had now released.

Apart from wild-bird trapping, he added, his biggest local problem was guard-dogs. The previous week he had had a case where one had been starved to death on a site near a technical college in South London. Some of the students had seen the dog, tried to feed it, but it had collapsed. In the end the dog had had to be put down. The site operator had been fined heavily, and warned by the magistrate that if he was convicted again, he would be banned completely from keeping guard-dogs.

On this particular afternoon, Kenny was going to investigate a complaint. Complaints can be called the bread-and-butter of the Inspector's day. Some may be groundless or even malicious, but they have to be investigated just the same. In fact, Kenny said he had a feeling that the one we were going to see just now could be fairly serious. Somebody had reported a dog being kept in a room of an upstairs flat in Poplar. According to the complainant it was never exercised, and the house was beginning to smell.

We turned off the Commercial Road, past some arches in a narrow alley that led down to Ratcliffe Highway. On the way we passed some garages and workshops, where a big Jamaican in a coloured shirt was sitting in the sun.

'How's that dog coming along?' asked Kenny.

'Fine.'

'He's eating fresh meat?'

'That dog eats nothing but fresh meat', said the Jamaican. 'He's looking fine.'

'If he looks as good as you do he's all right.' Kenny chuckled, said something incomprehensible and the Jamaican exploded with laughter. Afterwards Kenny told me he had served five years in the West Indies with the army, and learned the local dialect. 'It helps knowing it. If they get aggressive, I can talk a bit of the patois.' Kenny knows all the coloured churchmen in East Ham and gets them to put posters up in the Sunday Schools on animal care and education: 'Where they come from, dogs just roam around the street all day. I try to explain to them that bitches should be spayed, or at least not allowed to run free when they're in season.'

Presently we found the address that Kenny had been given about the complaint. It was a small terraced house in a sad little street where there was a lot of broken glass, boarded-up windows, and children playing.

Kenny knocked, and an old lady came to the door. 'You've come about the dog? He's upstairs.' There was no question as to whether it was the right place. You could smell it.

Prevention is better than cure.
Notice at a Pony Sale in the New Forest.

Keeping a safe distance downstairs, the old lady said the dog was never let out and barked all day. Kenny told her to stay in the kitchen while he had a look at it. As we went up the creaking stairway I asked him if he wouldn't be using the grasper, which is the long implement used by Inspectors for approaching a dangerous dog.

'Not unless I have to.' Kenny shook his head. 'The dog may have been hit with a stick some time – in that case he'll be frightened of the grasper. I want to try to examine him on his own terms.'

He pushed the door of the front room open a crack. Through it we could see the dog. He was a sandy sort of mongrel, with a touch of collie. He looked thin but not underfed. What was frightful was the smell, and the condition of the room. In one corner there was an old sideboard, with an empty saucer by it. Otherwise the room was completely strewn with rags and remnants of chewed-up cushions. There was also what looked at first sight like plaster, but was in fact excrement.

'It can't have been cleaned for months.' Kenny moved forward into the room, and I remembered what Mr. Butfield had said about all Inspectors having a sense of in-built anger. At first Kenny kept his distance from the dog, which was barking hoarsely. Then he knelt down, whistled softly and held his hand out.

'Come on, old feller. Come and see me.' He could have been talking to his own dog.

The dog made a bounding movement. I flinched, but Kenny didn't. Suddenly it was there, sniffing his hand.

'There's a good boy. He's a good dog.' By now the dog had started wagging his tail, then shot back with a crashing movement to the sideboard and hid behind it. 'You don't want to take any notice of a dog wagging his tail', said Kenny good-humouredly. 'He'll still bloody bite you. Come on old feller.'

This time the dog loped slowly out from behind the barricade of the sideboard. Kenny moved into the room, now a long way from the safety of the door, and snapped his fingers. 'Come on, up. Let's have a look at you.' Standing in the middle of the room, he coaxed the dog to put its forepaws on his shoulders, then expertly ran his fingers down its backbone.

'He's lean, but he isn't starved. Down, boy.'

The sandy-haired mongrel went down obediently, as if despite the smell and squalor he wanted to show he could be well behaved.

By now he seemed to be enjoying our visit. It occurred to me how desperately boring his life must be, and I recalled reading in one of the accounts of Scott's last expedition, that the worst problem for the dogs had been the sheer boredom of snow and ice, the absence of activity and smells. Even so, I thought, it could hardly have been as bad as the situation of a dog shut in a solitary room in Poplar.

We closed the door and went downstairs. Kenny told the old lady he'd be back, and would try to do something.

'Is there', I asked, 'anything you can really do in a case like that?'

'You can't prove cruelty. You might think so, I might think so, but you couldn't. All I can do, is get the Public Health people – they'll get a warrant to enter the house because of the smell, and I'll go with them. Probably the Public Health man'll issue an order saying the place must be cleaned up.'

'And the dog?'

'We might be able to do something with him. I'll try to persuade the owner to let me take him. Strictly speaking, I've no authority to do so.' He grinned. 'All the same, I'll try. On a patch like this you've got to bend the rules a bit.'

I could see John Kenny's point: it seemed another useful attribute for an Inspector. We closed the door and went out into the smoky Poplar sunshine.

The Traveller's Day

What makes somebody want to become an RSPCA Inspector? When Frank Milner came out of the RAF he first became an ambulance driver at Blackburn in Lancashire. One day in 1953 he went to pick up a patient to take her to hospital: although she was desperately ill, the old lady didn't want to leave her old springer spaniel. 'The only way I could get her to go was to promise I'd take the dog myself', Frank Milner recalls. 'So I took him. At least she went into hospital happy. I used to go and see her there, and give her a running report on Sandy every week till the old lady died.'

One day somebody who knew something about the RSPCA told Milner he was in the wrong job. Milner thought about it, applied to the Society, and joined as a trainee Inspector. Today he is one of the nine Travelling Superintendents who look after each region of the country. His own area comprises most of Yorkshire, Northumberland, and Durham. In the course of the year he sees all his Inspectors about seven times, and deals with difficulties which can vary from tricky prosecutions to an Inspector's accommodation problem. A cheerful man with a pipe, he told me when I arrived at his home in York that he had to go that afternoon to see some gipsies who had been prosecuted

65

for cruelty to a pony. While he was talking, Sally, the large black dog of indeterminate breed that was lying on the carpet, opened an eye, gave me a quizzical look, and went back to sleep.

The telephone rang. It was a query from the Inspector at Derby about a farmer who was in jail. It wasn't anything to do with cruelty, but there was no one to feed his animals while he was in jail, so the local Inspector was having to do it. While Mr. Milner was sorting it out I asked Keith, his youngest son, how long they had had the dog Sally.

Keith said it must be about five years – Sally had been thrown out of a bedroom window and hit on the forehead with a spade. 'She had two legs and both forepaws broken. Dad found her locked up in a shed. She'd have died, if he'd been twenty-four hours later.'

Frank Milner came back from the phone, and looked at Sally. 'When she first came you could do that' – he cupped his fingers in a circle – 'round her waist. You couldn't do it round her tail now. She weighed fifteen pounds, and when we stood her on the lino she just slithered over. I looked at her. I had the needle in my hand. I thought, no, we'll give her a try.'

Sally stirred, gave him a look which might have been gratitude but seemed more likely to be interest in the possibility of a walk. Keith said he would take her when he came back from train-spotting, and Mr. Milner and I got in the car to go and see the gipsies. Presently we were beyond the walls and on the outskirts of the city, heading out towards the moors the other side of Skipton.

On the way he told me a bit more detail about the gipsies. He had known this particular family for quite a while, and a lot of them were real old Romany characters who always treated their horses well. So it had been a bit of a surprise about six weeks before, when a lady who lived near the camp had rung in to say that one of the horses owned by the family was in distress.

'I was a bit doubtful at first', said Frank Milner, 'because in my experience gipsies rarely treat their ponies very badly. But when I got down there, I knew. I could smell the wound before I saw it. They'd had a tight band round the horse's neck, and every time he'd raised his head it chafed him. I don't know how long he'd had it on, but the wound was three inches deep.'

'What did you do then?'

'The first thing I did was to radio for a vet, then get the police down. They took the lad who owned the horse down to the police station and questioned him. Normally all prosecutions go through Society's head-quarters, but sometimes you get a case where you need to act quickly

This horse, formerly on a milk round, would have been destroyed if it had not been for the RSPCA.

to prevent further cruelty. This was one of those cases. He was charged that morning. I pointed out the relevant bit of law under the 1911 Act, and laid information with the Magistrate's Clerk. That all happened at lunch time on one day – he was convicted next morning. Fined £25 and the vet's fee.'

Twenty-five pounds. . . . The penalties for cruelty, it seemed, were hardly punitive. 'What about the pony?'

'The magistrate said he was to stay in our care till he was better. We've no facilities for looking after a horse in York, so he went to the Animal Home at Hull.'

'And the situation is that he's now better?'

Superintendent Milner nodded. 'They're bringing him over from

Hull this morning. I went up to the camp yesterday, to make sure they'd get a proper padded halter.'

'What will you do if they haven't got the halter?'

'Then they won't get the pony back.' Mr. Milner stuck his pipe firmly between his teeth. Soon we were going down a rough track, where there were some fields, a stream, and a sort of clearing.

The first time you see a gipsy camp at close range you get the momentary impression that everyone is wearing fancy dress. We were hemmed in by a crowd of dark excited faces, all talking broad Yorkshire with a hint of something foreign. There were a couple of smouldering camp fires, and an old woman sitting leaning on a stick as if she were a statue. A gaunt-looking young man, wearing a cowboy hat, and with a complexion faintly orange like strong tea, came over. Despite his youth and wispy beard, there was something commanding about him.

Mr. Milner introduced him as the horse's owner. 'We're bringing your pony back, Bert.'

The news produced an excited jabber of sound. A black-haired woman, wearing a shawl, pushed forward.

'He wor bad. He wor bad, that hoss.' They all shook their heads, as if the horse being bad was a sort of natural misadventure.

Mr. Milner waited for all this to subside. 'Did you get the halter, Bert?'

'Ay. I've got it in t'caravan.' He slipped off to where the old woman still leant on her stick, and a couple of lurcher dogs were prowling. A swarthily pretty little girl pretended to take Mr. Milner's picture with a battered camera, and one of the other women laughed.

'T'pony's been at Hull, hasn't it?'

'How the hell did you know it had been at Hull?' Mr. Milner looked fascinated. 'I suppose you saw that in the crystal ball, did you?'

'I could tell you a few other things too.' Her dark eyes glittered with amusement. By now Bert had come back with the halter. It was made of a rough webbing material.

Mr. Milner looked at it, rubbing his fingers over the webbing. 'It's a lot better than you had before. But what it really needs is a pad.' What had happened before, he explained to me, was that the neck band had cut into the horse's neck, when he raised his head to sniff the mares in another field: a pad would protect the place where the wound had been.

'I'll get a pad from t'smith tomorrow.'

There was a murmur of general acclamation from everyone. A pad from the blacksmith would be just the thing. It didn't seem to occur to anyone that Bert could have got it sooner.

Presently there was the sound of a truck coming down the narrow lane. One of the small lads who had posted themselves as lookouts called out that the pony was coming. A big horse box with 'RSPCA Hull Branch' painted on the side swung cautiously round the stony entrance. Mr. Milner greeted the driver, then went round to the tailboard. About a dozen of the gipsies poked their heads in the door at the side, trying to get a glimpse of the pony, so it got nervous and started to bang the sides of the box. Mr. Milner held his hand up, so that the pony could see it over the tailboard.

'It steadies them if they've something to watch.' By now the driver had got the tailboard down. There was almost a hum of applause as Bert came down, leading the little stallion like a Derby winner.

The stallion sniffed the familiar encampment air, bared his teeth and whinnied. Across his neck you could see the ridge where the wound had been made by the neck band. It was a sharp cleft about half-way down, healed now, but with the remains of a scab still on it. There was a murmur of approval from the gipsies when they saw how well it had healed and one little man with a wrinkled face nodded. 'It wor bad. I admit it.' It was the first time I heard any of the gipsies acknowledge that the wound might have been their fault.

Bert slipped the new webbing halter over the pony's head, and we all followed into the field. The pony began to munch the grass before an admiring audience. Presently he sniffed the mares in the adjoining field and threw his head back.

'You'll need to get that pad tomorrow.' Mr. Milner looked serious, and Bert nodded.

'I'll get it tomorrow.' He was going to town tomorrow anyway, he said, to get the pony cut, which meant castrated.

'Ay. You'll need to get him cut.' Mr. Milner slipped into the vernacular with friendly ease. 'You'll be selling him soon, will you?'

'We'll probably take him over to Boroughbridge Fair next month.'

'Well. Look after him now. We'll be getting off.' Mr. Milner shook hands with Bert, and we made our way back to the car. Everyone gathered round and waved. You felt the return of the pony would be remembered through many a winter evening by the camp fire. As we turned out of the track we got a glimpse of him, still munching.

'Bert's had a short sharp lesson', said Mr. Milner. 'I don't think he'll forget it.'

'Then is that the end of the story?'

'Not quite. We'll keep an eye on Bert. Soon they'll be taking their horses up to Boroughbridge Fair. I'll tell the Inspector there to look out for him.' He paused to light his pipe. 'There'll be a lot of people watching for a little black Dales pony.'

'So the Society's almost like a sort of underground?'

'I don't know that I'd put it like that', said Frank Milner modestly. 'Let's say we keep our ears open.'

In a way it seemed the best part of the story. The Society cannot care for all suffering animals, but where it knows of one, it cares completely. No trouble is too great if it will ease the suffering caused by a wound on the neck of one small, black Dales pony.

3 : The Promotion of Kindness

'The objects of the Society shall be to promote kindness and to prevent or suppress cruelty to animals and to do all such lawful acts as the Society may consider to be conducive or incidental to the attainment of those objects.'

RSPCA, Rule 2

Society Portrait

'You might not believe it, but this is our sitting-room.'

Mrs. Lilian Olley looked round at a dense mass of collecting tins, roneoed newsletters, and a stack of RSPCA literature to be delivered. An amiably tough, forthright lady in her early sixties, she is the secretary of the local branch of the Society at Rochester, Kent. Although she had always been fond of animals, she said, she hadn't thought of joining the RSPCA until a local Inspector suggested she was the kind of person who both could and ought to help.

Since then she has made animal welfare in Rochester her life. Assisted by her husband, a retired carpenter, who regards the take-over of their small terraced house as an animal welfare outpost with cheerful tolerance, she has become practically a local legend as someone who helps both animals and people with brisk, unsentimental common sense.

Among other things she runs an animal register which finds homes for around 900 birds and animals a year. Each month she puts out a roneoed list of everything from cats to canaries for adoption. 'You wouldn't think people would want to get rid of a canary, but they do. Only the other day a man knocked on the door and said he'd got a five-year-old canary that didn't sing. He was going to get a new one that did, and he wanted a home for the old one. I said you couldn't just cast a living creature off like that, but it was no use. In the end we'll probably find a home for it. But it might take a bit of doing.'

Running the animal register is only a sideline to running the Rochester branch: the following week, Mrs. Olley said, a local school was holding a big summer fête. The branch had been invited to have a stall, and she had just ordered 500 balloons from Headquarters, each bearing the RSPCA slogan. 'You don't raise a lot of money from things like that, but it helps keep the name in front of the public.' Another thing that was happening the same weekend was a road safety competition for dog owners – she would have to remember to get a couple of collecting tins round to the Inspector for that.

Meanwhile the phone kept ringing. One person was willing to give a home to a collie puppy on Mrs. Olley's list. Someone else had found a fledgling sparrow in their garden and wanted to know how to feed it, and a third wanted to know which vets were on call in Rochester on Sundays.

In the intervals of the various telephone calls, Mrs. Olley told me a bit more about the branch itself. With around 200 members in a predominantly industrial and dockyard town, the branch is a medium-sized and not particularly well-heeled one. 'All the same, we pay for ourselves. We pride ourselves that any animal problem in Rochester is our problem.' Basically, the funds come from the annual flag day, from various special efforts like the Christmas Draw and Bazaar, and from a second-hand shop recently started in Rochester High Street, which made a profit for the branch of just on £900 in 1972.

How does the money get spent? Mrs. Olley explained that all branches have to pay an annual quota towards Headquarters' expenses. In the case of the Rochester branch this is £340, which in 1972 was almost exactly covered by the flag day takings. All other proceeds go to various forms of animal welfare in the district – the largest item in 1972 being the voucher system, which provides free veterinary treatment for pets whose owners – particularly pensioners – could not otherwise afford it.

Balloons and collecting tins and roneoed newsletters may seem the small change of charitable work. All the same, the RSPCA could not exist without them.

Nor could it exist without its Mrs. Olleys. A hundred and fifty years ago the national conscience towards suffering animals was represented by twenty or so people who met in the Coffee House in London. Today that conscience is represented by a great many thousand people who meet in halls and committee rooms throughout the country.

*

Meanwhile the branches are only one part of the story. Let us begin by taking a look at the organization as a whole. We can get a rough initial picture by seeing the Society as made up of two strands. First there is the Headquarters strand, consisting of the professional staff now based at Horsham under the Executive Director, Major Ronald Seager.

Basically the Horsham staff are the people who handle the day-to-day work of the Society – the Inspectors, the Veterinary officers, the legal side, education, the appeals staff, and the people in charge of animal homes throughout the country. One of the most important departments is Clinics, which runs two large animal hospitals in London, as well as a series of smaller branch clinics and animal welfare centres. Besides these the department is responsible for four mobile clinics in North and South Wales, Northumberland, and Cornwall, which bring a weekly service to remote rural areas. The Legal Department not only looks after the Society's own legal affairs, including bequests, but also handles prosecutions. The smallest, but one of the most important departments is the Parliamentary Liaison Office, in touch with M.P.s over Bills affecting animal welfare.

There, for the moment, we can leave the professional side. The second strand is made up of the members, and particularly the active ones in the branches. Anyone over eighteen can become a member of the RSPCA. At the time of writing the Society has 65,000, each of whom pays £1 for a year's subscription. Not all are active members: for those who want to be, the obvious nucleus is their local branch. There are 207 branches spread over England and Wales, supported by 3,317 supporting units known as auxiliaries. Mostly based on smaller towns or villages, these exist as satellites to the main branches.

The first thing you notice about the branches is that none is quite like another. One branch may rely on the traditional flag day, while another will have a reputation for elaborate schemes of fund-raising. Another branch might run an animal home in the district, perhaps one which concentrates on wildlife.

Increasingly the most effective branches are those which see their work as part of an across-the-board social service. One branch chairman told me of a case where helping the animals had been a way of helping people. 'This particular family had four cats, to which they were all devoted. Then the man had to go into hospital for a major operation, as a result of which he wasn't going to be able to work, and he certainly wasn't going to be able to afford to keep four cats in cat food. The family decided they'd have to put them down – on the other hand what was that man going to say when he came out of hospital and found all his cats gone? It would have broken his heart.' The happy ending to the story is that the branch arranged to supply free pet food to the family, and are still doing so as I write.

Branches at work. It may be a stand at the County Show –

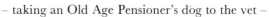

– taking an Old Age Pensioner's dog to the vet –

– or organizing a Christmas bazaar.

On the other hand there are branches – and many people in the Society see this as the biggest problem – which are frankly moribund. 'Individualism's all very well,' said one RSPCA Council member, Mrs. Angela Cope, 'but what do you do when you get a branch clinic where they've got distemper in the kennels, yellowing posters on the walls, and a branch secretary who won't give up? Sooner or later, there'll have to be some sort of standardization for the branches.'

Partly this variation in the branches is the result of a long tradition of virtual branch autonomy. Until after the first World War, there were many independent SPCAs, existing side by side with local branches of the Society. It was not until the 1930s that even such large cities as Birmingham, Sheffield and Newcastle gave up their independence. Walsall, the last independent SPCA, did not join forces with the RSPCA until 1948.

Even today, few branches make any contribution to central funds apart from the annual levy. If somebody leaves a legacy naming the

75

Gala Performances help the Society's work.
H.R.H. Princess Alexandra talks to Frankie Howerd.
With them, Council member David Jacobs and Cliff Richard.

RSPCA, it will go to what is known as the Headquarters account. But many other bequests will be left to local branches. When this happens, the branch may put the money to something like a dogs' home, or buying an animal ambulance for their district. Alternatively there is nothing to stop them leaving it in the bank, sometimes to the irritation of Headquarters, which could well use the money for better clinics, education or more Inspectors. The branches, for their part, have been known to make dark muttering noises about 'money going to London'.

Such rugged regional individualism may be healthy for both parties – meanwhile how do the branches fit into the organization as a whole?

Basically, the governing body of the RSPCA is its Council, whose meetings are held every month in London.

At the moment the Council consists of forty-six people, twenty-four of whom are elected by all the members, sixteen by the branches, and the rest co-opted. Any member of the Society can put up for the Council, provided he can get a proposer, seconder, and the support of ten other members. 'The ten member rule was brought in to keep the cranks out', said one member. 'It doesn't always work.'

Even so, the present composition of the RSPCA Council is not noticeably cranky. Among the forty-six there are Members of Parliament from both main parties, and several distinguished scientists. There is also Nadia Nerina, the ballet star, David Jacobs from television, and Richard Meade the Olympic show-jumping Gold Medallist.

Membership of the General Council means a good deal more than merely attending a monthly meeting: most members will receive huge amounts of paper work and correspondence. Apart from being likely

Fund-raising activities included an evening at the Tower of London in 1972. *Left to right*, the Lady Mayoress; Angela Cope, Chairman of Central London branch; the Lord Mayor; Olympic Gold Medallists Mary Peters and Richard Meade; and John Hobhouse, Chairman of the Society.

to be involved with their local branch, they will almost certainly sit on one of the standing committees which look after Clinics, Education, Publicity, Overseas, Branches or Homeless Animals.

Basically, it is these committees which provide the link between ordinary members and the professional staff who plan and attend all meetings: in most cases there is an active and very close co-operation between Council members and the department heads from Horsham. The system may seem, as one branch secretary said, a bit like a pre-war county cricket team with the amateurs running the professionals, but it seems to work. 'One thing you've got to remember about the Society', I was told, 'is that it could never survive without idealism. Of course the professional and technical skills come from the staff. But the other side of the coin will always be the devotion of Council members.'

Often the members also contribute some particular talent or expertise. Nadia Nerina, for example, devised and organizes the special Gala Performances in aid of the Society, while the Overseas Committee is chaired by Sir John Ward, formerly ambassador to Turkey and Brazil: his predecessor was the distinguished former Colonial Governor, Sir Charles Woolley. Members of Parliament on the Council will be consulted on matters relating to legislation. Those who are veterinary surgeons provide a valuable link with such bodies as the British Veterinary Association and the Royal College.

Many chairmen of committees do a working stint which would seem arduous if they were getting paid for it. The chairman of the Animal Homes Committee, for example, will be likely to visit every one of the sixty-nine dogs' homes in the country during a year. To take one example of the kind of work put in by Council members, Mrs. Angela Cope has sat on every sub-committee of the Council. Currently she is not only chairman of the Publicity and Appeals Committee, but also runs the central London branch. Hardly a day goes by when she is not involved in some Society activity, whether it is collecting items for a jumble sale or working through several hundred paintings entered for a children's competition. 'Over the years', said one of the London branch helpers, 'she must have raised hundreds of thousands for the Society.'

Over the last few years the man mainly responsible for guiding the Council's strategy has been a tall, greying, almost excessively handsome West-country Liberal named John Hobhouse. Both his grandfather and great grandfather were Liberal cabinet ministers. An earlier Whig ancestor was John Cam Hobhouse, the friend of Byron and one of the main supporters of the great Reform Bill.

Despite the family reforming tradition, Hobhouse had no particular

A meeting of the RSPCA Council. For a list of members in the Anniversary Year, *see* Appendix I.

The Animal Experimentation Committee meets. *Left to right*, Mike Seymour-Rouse (Publicity and Appeals); Douglas Houghton, M.P.; Bill Jordan (Veterinary Department); Dr. Kit Pedler; Richard Sayer (Parliamentary Liaison).

interest in animal welfare in his youth. 'I was brought up in the normal country routine of killing everything you saw', he admits. Then he met the daughter of a local country doctor who combined, as Hobhouse says, 'a considerable knowledge of cuneiform hieroglyphics with an absolute conviction that animals and humans had the same basic right to live.'

When Hobhouse married the doctor's daughter, his interest in animals underwent what he calls a profound change. He adopted two stray dogs, joined the Bath branch of the RSPCA, and gave up fishing and sold his guns. 'You see enough suffering in the RSPCA', he said, 'without adding to it.' Before long he and his wife had built up the local animal home at Bath, where his family business is in the toy trade. Despite his business commitments and having to spend at least two days a week in London for the Society, he is still actively concerned with the local branch. He sees the Inspector there three times a week, and now has five dogs of his own – all strays from the local dogs' home.

Hobhouse stresses that this kind of experience in branch work is the essential groundwork of being a member of the Council – indeed one of his own first actions on being elected was to help set up the Homeless Animals Committee. Among other campaigns he helped stop the export of Irish horses to the continent, and also prepared a pamphlet on animal experimentation which led to 119 questions being asked in Parliament, and to the eventual setting-up of a Government Committee.

Hobhouse's name seems likely to go down in the Society's history as its first great reforming Chairman. One of his earliest actions on taking office in 1969 was to start a new policy of bringing in higher-powered staff. Another example of the stress on professionalism came with the introduction in 1971 of a series of specialist committees. 'Committees may sound dull,' says John Hobhouse, 'but the point of these was that they were bringing in new kinds of experts. If you're going to put a case to a team of high-powered Government scientists, it's not much use sending along a deputation of kindly ladies in flowered hats. You've got to have people they'll regard as scientific equals.'

The first specialist committee, that on Factory Farming, was set up under the chairmanship of Professor John Napier, a distinguished anthropologist from London University: in its second year it held a symposium of world experts on the subject, and has already commissioned, for the first time in the Society's history, its own research. Since then other committees have been set up on Wild Life and Animal Experimentation: the latter, particularly, has been able to put the case against unnecessary experiments for the first time on a scientific level.

But perhaps the area where Hobhouse has most persistently improved

80

relations is that where many people feel the Society to be weakest – in communications between Headquarters and the branches. 'Before he arrived', said one branch secretary, 'we existed in a sort of limbo. If we had to approach Headquarters for something, it was a bit like writing to the Kremlin. If some of the previous Chairmen had turned up at a local branch meeting, nobody would have known them.' It is the measure of Hobhouse's success that he is now universally known: since 1969 he had indefatigably toured the country, speaking at the Annual General Meeting of many remote rural branches as well as urban ones.

Meanwhile there is one other aspect of John Hobhouse's time as Chairman which has attracted what some members would say was more than its share of public interest. This, to which we must now turn, is the long, rumbling and divisive row over fox-hunting.

A Brush with Conscience

Perhaps the most surprising thing about the debate over fox-hunting is that it is a relatively modern issue. For centuries Englishmen had hunted wild animals from deer to otters, and deemed it their right to do so. Few would have disagreed with Gilbert White of Selborne, who said that most men were sportsmen by constitution. 'There is such an inherent spirit for hunting in human nature', he said, 'as scarce any inhibitions can restrain.'

Even by the early nineteenth century there were few protesting voices. There is no mention of hunting in the early records of the Society – there were, after all, many more obvious cruelties to be dealt with. Often the hunters were, or would have said they were, animal-lovers. 'I have known', said the Revd. Henry Crowe, writing in 1824, 'many men possessing true principles of benevolence and moral obligation, who join, and with keenness, in the sports of the field. Yet I must be allowed to say, that this is done during the slumber of reason . . .'

By the turn of this century there were still many of the Society's supporters who saw no contradiction in enjoying hunting. Among them was Dr. Edmond Warre, the Headmaster of Eton, which still retained its pack of beagles. Criticized by another humane society, the Humanitarian League, Dr. Warre replied that he had never been given to understand that the RSPCA condemned the hunting of animals. 'If it does,' he added, 'ought it not at once to enlighten its subscribers upon this point so that they may not be contributing to its funds under a false impression?'

Meanwhile the number of abolitionists was growing. One of those most contemptuous of the Society's failure to condemn hunting was the Hon. Stephen Coleridge, himself a Council member and Secretary of the National Anti-Vivisection Society. 'The excuse commonly proffered by the Council', he wrote, 'is that it would lose the support and subscriptions and bequests of its more conservative members, among whom it reckons the mighty hunters of stags, foxes, hares and otters.'

All the same the Society was beginning to take some small but active steps. In 1909, partly as the result of pressure from Coleridge himself, it supported the Humanitarian League in an attempt to ban the Royal Buckhounds in Windsor Forest. In 1910 Gilbert Murray, later to be President of the Society, was one of a group of university professors who supported an anti-hunting Bill put forward in the Commons. In 1921, when the Society decided to take a poll of its members on the question of deer-hunting, the vote was three to one for abolition.

But it was not until the early 1930s that hunting began to become a deeply divisive issue. In 1926 the League Against Cruel Sports was formed, rising from the ashes of the old Humanitarian League: four years later it was joined by another body, the National Society for the Abolition of Cruel Sports. The RSPCA, meanwhile, continued to take action in the Parliamentary field. In 1930 it helped Lovat Fraser, M.P., to present a Bill to end deer-hunting. The Bill failed; so, more remarkably, did a prosecution brought by the Society two years later when a carted deer was hunted into the Channel by the Mid-Kent Staghounds, and had to be rescued by the Hythe lifeboat.

In 1949 Seymour Cocks, M.P., was successful in the Private Members' Ballot. Helped by the Society, he prepared a Bill to outlaw both deer- and otter-hunting as well as coursing. The Labour government of the day, possibly mindful both of a coming election and the rural vote, failed to support the Bill, which was defeated by more than 100 votes. The government then set up a Committee of Inquiry under J. Scott-Henderson, Q.C. Reporting in 1951, the Committee made no proposals to ban any form of hunting. The Protection of Animals Act, they said, did not apply to hunting except where unnecessary suffering was inflicted.

Six years after the Scott-Henderson Committee, the RSPCA came out with the firmest statement it had made so far. It was, it said, opposed to the hunting of wild deer with hounds, to carted stag-hunting, to coursing, and the hunting of otters and badgers. It was also opposed to the involvement of children in all forms of hunting. On the specific issue of fox-hunting the statement was more equivocal. Though the

Society was categorically against any kind of hunting for sport, it said, alternative methods of keeping foxes down might cause more suffering.

In the eyes of the more ardent abolitionists, this did not go far enough: what they wanted was a total condemnation of all forms of hunting. As long as the Society even appeared to tolerate hunting as a means of control, they said, the hunting lobby could point to the fact that the Society was not against it.

Some abolitionists went much further. Supporters of hunting, they claimed, had been allowed to infiltrate the Society, and even become Council members. As evidence of this, they quoted letters which had appeared in various hunting publications, urging their supporters to join the RSPCA. At the Annual General Meeting in 1968, the abolitionists pointed out, a group of field sports supporters had packed the hall, outvoted an anti-hunting resolution, then left the meeting with horns blaring.

The 1970 Annual General Meeting produced still more ferocious wranglings between abolitionists and the Council. Gathering in a North London primary school afterwards, fifteen Society members decided that the time had come for action. It is worth noting that, of the fifteen, few corresponded to the traditional style of the Society's supporters: for example, John Bryant, a 28-year-old helicopter engineer from Yeovil, had first found himself to be an animal-lover when he had gone round as a boy with a local gang in the back streets. 'I was', he says, 'always the one who was stopping then running down cats with pushbikes.' Within a couple of months the Reform Group, as it became known, had been established with the declared object of restoring the Society to the anti-cruelty principles from which, in the Group's view, it had deviated by even appearing to tolerate hunting.

Probably there is no theme calculated to engender quite such acrimony as that of bloodsports. From the first, the Reform Group's salvoes came in terms of personal attack on members of the General Council said to have links with hunting organizations. WAS THERE IN FACT A PLOT? asked one pamphlet, referring to the alleged infiltration by huntsmen. Whatever case the Reform Group had, many members felt, was not likely to be helped by the generally aggressive tone. 'The trouble with the Reform Group', says one Council member not unsympathetic to their cause, 'is that they always wanted confrontations, not negotiations. The other thing they didn't realize is that most of the Council have spent most of their lives promoting animal welfare. Naturally, they didn't take kindly to being called hypocrites and plotters.'

Not all the acrimony came from one side. In the overheated atmosphere, there was even argument over the name of Mr. Brian Seager, who succeeded John Bryant as the Reform Group's chairman. When members received the Group's propaganda signed by Mr. Seager, said the Council, they could easily mistake it for official literature sent by the Society's Executive Director, Major Ronald Seager. The Reform Group replied, not without logic, that Mr. Seager could hardly be expected to change his name, but the row continued.

In 1971 something approaching a total breach came after a meeting between members of the Group and members of the Council. The meeting had made it obvious, said the RSPCA's chairman, that the Group's 'apparent obsession with plots and charges . . . made it a waste of time to hold further talks . . . Further communications from the Reform Group will remain unanswered.'

Since then the debate has continued with unmatched vigour. A new controversy arose when Princess Anne went hunting on two or three winter weekends. Reform Group members put out a press statement which suggested, somewhat optimistically, that the Queen as Patron of the Society should express public disapproval of the fact that her daughter had ridden to hounds. The episode helped to swing moderate opinion against the Group, especially as it came in the middle of the campaign to stop the export of live food animals to Europe. 'It was a disastrous piece of timing', said one rural branch secretary, himself opposed to hunting, who had to address a SELFA meeting just after the Princess Anne story had made news. 'How the hell do you explain a situation like this to an audience of farmers?'

Such vituperation apart, how much truth is there in the Reform Group's claims? The Council's answer to charges of infiltration by huntsmen is that the allegations are patently untrue. Richard Meade, the Olympic show jumper, is the only member of the RSPCA Council who hunts and he, the Council says, was specially co-opted in order to improve relations with the British Horse Society. Another co-opted member, Frederick Burden, M.P. for Gillingham, holds an honorary position in a group of Kent wildfowlers. Mr. Burden, added the Society's quarterly magazine, *RSPCA Today*, in an acid comment, 'has probably achieved a great deal more for animal welfare than the whole of the self-styled Reform Group put together'. Where the Reform Group may have a case, some members think, is in a more subtle area: rightly or wrongly, there is a feeling that some Council members, because of their social backgrounds, are likely to be on friendly terms with hunting people. 'Of course there haven't been plots', I was told. 'That isn't to say there isn't a sort of intuitive Old Boy network.'

One Council criticism which Reform Group members feel is less than fair is the much-repeated claim that they are only concerned with bloodsports. Out of eleven Reform Group sympathizers on the RSPCA Council, John Bryant points out, one is an expert on factory farming, another on vivisection, another is a Labour M.P. who has worked extensively for animal welfare bills in Parliament, Bryant himself works every Sunday cleaning out kennels and catteries at a local sanctuary in Dorset. Celia Hammond, though she was elected on a Reform Group ticket, primarily put up for the Council because she wanted to influence the Society to mount a bigger campaign on cat-neutering, which she regards as a far more important issue.

If a little of the heat can be taken out of the discussion, will the Reform Group ultimately be seen to have made a positive contribution? Today's rebels can have a way of being tomorrow's leaders, but what many middle-of-the road members fear is that a more powerful Reform Group could lead to the Society's becoming a completely different kind of organization. 'There's a need', one branch secretary told me, 'for the Society to be very professional and very balanced. We've got to have a broad front line for animal welfare. If you allow it to be taken over by a group with one specific aim, the whole spectrum of our work could be affected.'

Perhaps the most optimistic – and one hopes, realistic – view came from one Council member who said that what the Society needed was more, not less discussion. 'Because of the Reform Group', he said, 'we're getting younger, more vigorous people on the Council. The other thing people say is that the publicity is bad for the Society, but in my view it isn't. When you've got a Society that stands for principles the British people on the whole agree with, then all publicity is good.'*

Meanwhile there is one character who tends to get a bit left out of the story, and that is the fox himself. Have the events of the last three

---

* Such a view may seem a little hopeful in the light of the publicity arising from the Inquiry held at the Seymour Hall, in London, in January 1974, when members of the Society were invited to put their views on its management and constitution to an independent Panel chaired by Mr. Charles Sparrow, Q.C. One of the criticisms was the frequently repeated one that the Council had been infiltrated by fox-hunters. Another was that dogs were being put down in circumstances somewhat melodramatically compared to Nazi death camps. Though all such criticisms were rebutted by the Society, there is no doubt that much damage was done to the RSPCA's collective image – and not least to the kind of people whose dedicated and self-sacrificing work is described in this book. The other rather sad conclusion to be drawn from the Inquiry is that if there is perhaps one virtue conspicuously absent among some animal lovers, it is a sense of proportion.

years brought the Reform Group's main object – the abolition of hunting – any nearer? Certainly there would be massive rejoicing in the Society if another means of control could be found. Another solution might come from the special committee recently set up by the Society to study the habits of the fox, among other forms of wildlife. If it should be shown that he is less of a predator than is generally believed, it could get the Society off a hook which many people wish it had never got on.

Cleo, Pure Dog

Let me declare my interest straight away and say I have a special attachment to the Liverpool branch of the RSPCA. I first went there before I started to write this book: I had been doing some preliminary research, and stopped there briefly on my way to see the North Wales mobile clinic. In the course of a short visit, I had gone round the branch's dogs' home with the branch secretary, a genial character named Bill Stabback. He had taken me down what seemed a labyrinth of kennels – narrow asphalt paths between rows and rows of wire cages. As we entered each block there came a barrage of barking. There were black dogs, brown dogs, small dogs, big dogs. There were dogs that looked pleading, dogs that looked insulted; and there were small, curled-up dogs that simply lay there. It was a sort of fantasia on a theme of dogs. Raising my voice to be heard above the barking, I asked Bill Stabback where they came from.

'Mostly they're police strays. We've got the biggest dog problem in the country here. Five thousand dogs a year brought in off the street. And another 6,000 to be found homes for.'

'What on earth do you do with them?'

'We keep them all eight days. A few of the strays get claimed by the owners. If not, anyone can take them.'

'And if nobody takes them?'

'Then I'm afraid they get put down. In Liverpool we're putting down something like 7,000 every year.'

I looked at him. Seven thousand dogs a year. It sounded more like a massacre than anything to do with a humane society.

'It sounds grim, I know, but what else can you do? The trouble is you've got so many women going out to work. They don't want the dog messing on the carpet, so they put it on the street at nine o'clock when the kids go to school, and hope for the best. If they come home and find the dog on the doorstep, then well and good. If he's not there, he's either lost, or he's mating somewhere, meaning more pups on the way.'

Cleo, pure dog.

We walked down a few more corridors of kennels. The fantasia on a theme of dogs had turned to a darker variation. Bill Stabback stroked a big Alsatian's nose. While he was doing so, I noticed a small dog in the next kennel. It wasn't doing anything in particular, and it certainly wasn't a describable breed – just brown and black and rather small. It might have had a bit of fox terrier, even a faint trace of Alsatian. If you had to call it anything, you would have said pure dog.

'Surely someone'll adopt that one?'

'You'd think so.' Bill Stabback put his finger to the wire and the little dog nuzzled up and licked it. He consulted a card on the cage. On the card it had the initials T.B.F.H. and a date. He looked at it, then turned to me. 'That means To Be Found Home. She's been here a week. She'll be put down if nobody's taken her by tomorrow.'

I wouldn't say I thought a lot about the little dog between Liverpool and Wales – after all, wasn't it merely sentimental to be concerned about one animal out of several hundred? There were worse things going on in the world, I told myself, than unwanted dogs being destroyed.

Even so when I rang up home that evening, I was still thinking about the little brown and black face.

'How did you get on?' my wife said on the phone.

'All right', I said. 'I nearly brought home a dog.'

'Why didn't you?' As it happened we didn't have a dog at the moment.

All the same, I thought, no. The dog might have been ill-treated by someone – with a three-year-old at home, we didn't want an animal that might prove vicious. Next afternoon I set off for London. Probably someone would have taken her by now. If not, she might already have been put down. There were a lot of good reasons, but the thought of that little face kept coming back.

Even so I don't think I really meant to do anything about it until I got to a roundabout where the road divided. One road was for Chester, the shortest route for London. The other was marked Liverpool. I drove round the roundabout twice, then somehow, I'm still not sure how, found myself not on the Chester road but heading for Liverpool.

An hour later I was sitting, somewhat to his surprise, in Bill Stabback's office. 'We hadn't expected to see you back so soon', he said. 'Did you leave something behind?'

'Yes. That little mongrel bitch. If she's still here, I've come to take her.'

Probably you can guess the rest of the story. That afternoon I drove down the motorway with the little dog in the back of the car, her nose peering out of a cardboard container. I think the bearded student I gave a lift to was rather surprised when I said I'd happily take him as far as Birmingham if he'd sit in the back as a dog-sitter, but he did. When I got home, the children called her Cleo.

We have had Cleo over a year now, and a sweeter-natured dog would be hard to imagine. Sometimes I tell her that if she is naughty I will send her back to Knotty Ash. Only she never is naughty. People sometimes ask what breed she is. We always say pure dog.

The Urban Problem

Apart from Cleo I had another special reason for wanting to go back to Liverpool, for the branch there is the oldest in the country. Even before the meeting at Old Slaughter's Coffee House there had been an attempt to set up a humane society on Merseyside. The only record we have of it is in an advertisement in a paper impressively named

88

The Liverpool Branch: the animal home at Edge Lane.

Billinger's Liverpool Advertiser & Marine Intelligencer. On 6 November 1809, it announced, a meeting would take place at the *Crown and Anchor* Inn in Bold Street, with the object of forming a society 'for the Suppression of Wanton Cruelty to Animals'. The presence of gentlemen interested in such a cause, added the advertisement, was urgently requested.

Three weeks later another meeting was held, but thereafter there is silence till 1825. By this time the London Society already existed, and in the Minutes of 11 April 1825 Arthur Broome reported to the London committee 'that a correspondent Society seemed to be in progress at Liverpool'. In 1834 another advertisement appeared in the *Liverpool Mercury*. This time it announced the official formation of a society which would 'chiefly direct its attention to the prevention of cruel practices towards animals, particularly those killed for the food of man'.

Such were the earliest origins. In the years that followed there seems to have been little contact between activities in Liverpool and those in London. In 1872 there were apparently two groups in Liverpool: a purely independent local society and a branch of the RSPCA.

To judge from the early Minute books and newspaper records, there was not much love lost between them. In 1872 we find one group making scathing references to 'flamboyant advertisements', inserted in the Liverpool press by the other. In the same year the Liverpool Inspector was removed, much to the annoyance of local members.

Possibly some of the trouble may have been a certain patrician attitude, for the Liverpool branch seems to have been an upper-class preserve. In 1872, we read that the selection of a branch chairman was to be made from a list comprising two earls, a lord, a baronet, the Lord Mayor of Liverpool, and two bishops. Even in the hints on stopping cruelty, a somewhat lordly attitude can be detected: 'Servants should be admonished if inflicting pain . . . a rebuke should be given to costermongers, donkey-keepers, and goat-drivers.' No doubt such advice was well-intentioned, but one wonders how much it helped the animals.

Liverpool clinic manager Brian Maltby with a new arrival.

By 1873 the breach, whatever it had been, was apparently healed. Both local societies decided to amalgamate, and to come under the umbrella of the main society in London. The collaboration was clearly fruitful. In April 1881 we find the *Liverpool Daily Post* saying in a leader that the Society 'had no more valuable and active branch than that located in this city. It is evidence of the careful and prudent manner in which the cases are conducted, that out of nearly five hundred prosecutions only four failed for lack of evidence.'

Prosecutions were the main work, but on the positive side we find the Ladies' Committee in 1885 awarding prizes to cabdrivers for their general good conduct and kindness to their horses. 'Woollen jackets', noted the *Daily Post*, 'were also presented to eight of the most deserving donkey drivers, to encourage them in treating their donkeys with consideration.'

These records are worth glancing at in a little detail because they show on what solid foundations the Liverpool tradition is built. Today the branch has 2,500 members, runs the large animal home behind Littlewoods' building in Edge Lane, and is due to open a new custom-built clinic as part of a new community centre at Everton. In addition it runs a horses' home, quarantine and boarding kennels at Halewood, and another clinic at the new town at Kirkby, where the local council approached the branch and offered them free accommodation if the Society would provide a service.

This is only one example of the extent to which the branch co-operates with local bodies. If old-age pensioners are going into hospital, their pets must be looked after: the local Social Welfare services contact the branch, who arrange free boarding at the Halewood kennels. When Liverpool Corporation were building a new community centre at Everton, they saw an animal clinic as essential. In response to their request, the branch opened a new clinic at Richmond Terrace, which maintains a twenty-four-hour service for emergency calls, with free daily sessions where animals get expert treatment.

But essentially the problem in Liverpool is the sheer numbers of unwanted cats and dogs. When I went back to see Bill Stabback he said it was, if anything, slightly worse than at the time when I had taken Cleo. In addition to the problem of wives going out to work and putting the dog on the street, there were more high-rise blocks and shopping precincts. 'A new shopping precinct is very nice to look at, but it's a menace for attracting dogs.'

It is hard to see how the urban dog problem could be coped with at all if it were not for the RSPCA. Every morning a van drives out from Edge Lane on what the drivers call the milk round. They may have to visit any or all of the twenty-four police stations in the area to bring in the stray dogs from overnight. If the police want to hand over an animal direct, there is a special kennel at Edge Lane to which they have a key. They can drive up, leave the dog in the kennel which has a bed, with food and water ready. In the morning when the staff arrive, the dog will be booked in.

Probably few people know that the police in almost every town will hand stray dogs over to the Society as a matter of course. Because it is technically still their responsibility, the police pay the branch for keeping the dog the statutory eight days. If, at the end of that time, nobody has claimed it, then the Society must either find a home for the dog or destroy it.

Currently the Liverpool and Bootle police pay the branch £13,500 a year for this service, and it will be much more when, at the request of the new Merseyside County Council, Southport and the Wirral area is also taken over. Bill Stabback told me the figure does not anything like cover the cost of staff and maintaining the kennels, but it helps. If the Society was not there, the police would have to do their own destroying.

What happens in the happier cases when a dog can be found a home? Any apparently responsible adult may take a dog, but Bill Stabback and his staff will be careful to see that no animal is taken to be used as a guard-dog for a site unless the operator will look after it properly. It is a grim reminder of the toughness of urban life that one of the kennel staff told me that, in his view, most dogs were taken because so many people wanted watch-dogs. 'A lot of the people who come here', he said, 'aren't buying a dog. They're buying a cheap burglar alarm. The dog we're most asked for is an Alsatian.'

*

When I started writing this book, one tender-hearted lady said to me, 'You won't forget the cats, will you?' It is hard to forget cats in Liverpool. In 1972 the branch found homes for 760 out of just on 8,000 strays, and had to have the rest destroyed. A few cats come from their owners, many more from areas where demolition of old houses is going on and people simply leave their cats behind. Wild cats are not merely a problem but a danger around factory canteens, derelict areas, and the docks.

Because of Liverpool's cat problem, two of the best-known figures in the city are Olive Burns and Ivy Gosney, two of the branch staff-drivers. Known locally as the 'Olly and the Ivy, they are particularly respected by the Liverpool dockers who have seen them catching wild cats, usually without a grasper. During the month I met them, Olive Burns said, they had collected 955 cats, mostly from slum clearance areas.

Some of their stories are frightful. One day Ivy Gosney went into a big department store in the city and saw a man in the shoe department opening a box of sandals. 'It contained four kittens – clearly they'd been put there by someone who wanted to get rid of them, but couldn't or wouldn't have them put down properly.' Olive Burns said people will do anything with cats – dump them, or throw them out of cars on the East Lancashire Road. If the branch takes a cat to be destroyed it charges a collection fee of 40p. To avoid paying this, some people will hand over their own pet as a stray, which isn't charged for. 'You'll get a call to pick up a stray', says Olive Burns. 'When you get there the children will cry and say "They're taking away our cat."'

How does the Liverpool branch maintain its service? In the past, a large part of the funds had come from legacies, Bill Stabback told me. 'Even in 1972 we had a total number of legacies amounting to £33,000. In the first six months of 1973, there were none.'

If, as seems likely with rising death duties and less inherited wealth, the supply of legacies dries up, how will the branch maintain its various services and the employment of over fifty people? One answer, Bill Stabback said, could be the help of a professional fund-raiser, who had been appointed and would soon be starting work. Few of the facilities could survive on the proceeds of the Christmas Draw and Flag Day, with a combined total of £1,700.

In the meantime the branch continues to rely on a devoted staff – people like Brian Maltby, the 30-year-old Superintendent of the dogs' home, who gave up a job as a factory manager to work here for half the money. When I asked him why, he said that if you felt you wanted to work in any kind of welfare there wasn't really a choice. 'You need the job', he said, 'as much as the job needs you.'

Why, I asked, work with animals? Brian said that he felt involved with a lot of different kinds of social service, but felt that handling animals was his *métier*. 'I couldn't work with children who someone had been cruel to. I'd think of my own children and get too emotionally involved.'

Before I left Liverpool I went round the kennels I had seen on my previous visit – the same long lines of wire cages, asphalt paths, the same sad barking of so many dogs. The saddest of all the rooms in Edge Lane is the destruction room, with its racks of black metal boxes. There

A new home for a Liverpool stray – complete with lead and licence.

was something posted on the wall I had remembered and wanted to copy down – the reminder to the staff that all destructions should be done with gentleness and kindness.

Brian Maltby and I went into the darkened room. Most of the boxes were empty, but in one there was a small expiring kitten, its crime to have been born in a city with too many cats.

We went over to the notice on the wall and I copied the words down. 'A kindly word or touch may do much to comfort and reassure. . . . If the animal is a savage one, remember that condition has been brought on by man's inhumanity.'

'That's very true.' Brian Maltby nodded. 'No animal's in its nature vicious. It's people that make it so.'

'Do you ever get case-hardened?'

'I wouldn't say case-hardened. You get detached, because you have to. If we didn't, we'd all be having nervous breakdowns.' Brian said he had a Yorkshire terrier he had taken from the home. It had had its jaw broken by being kicked. For six months after he took it home it had been terrified. It still winced if you accidentally moved your foot near it.

We walked back past the lines of dogs and through to Brian's office. As we went in one of the kennel girls was waiting with a query. It seemed someone had been asking if a home could be found for a white poodle.

'As a matter of fact we can.' Brian looked suddenly delighted. 'A very good home too. The father-in-law of Joe Mercer, the Coventry City manager. He had a white poodle before – now he's looking for another. I'll ring him straight away.'

I left Brian to make his cheerful telephone call and said goodbye. It seemed a good note to end up on. The Liverpool Dogs' Home sees a little happiness and a lot of heartbreak. In the end the animals are only part of it. The story of a suffering animal is often also the story of a degraded human.

Branch Lines Open

Geographically or spiritually you cannot get much farther in England from the East Lancashire Road than Bosinney. Bosinney is a small hamlet just outside Tintagel in Cornwall. Once it returned Sir Francis Drake as one of its two Members to Parliament, and more recently gave John Galsworthy, who lived near by, the name of Irene's lover in the *Forsyte Saga*.

I had gone to Bosinney to meet a man named Michael Williams. The East Cornwall branch of which he is secretary, I had been told, was one of the most go-ahead and thriving in the West Country.

Michael Williams turned out to be an ebullient ex-journalist with an overflow of both energy and high spirits. He needs both – in addition to the East Cornwall branch he runs the local hotel, a small publishing house of his own, and, almost as dear to his heart as the RSPCA, a cricket club called the Cornish Crusaders.

What, I asked, had first got him involved with the Society? Michael Williams explained that he had always been fond of animals and had joined around five years ago. A little later the branch secretary had been giving up and someone had suggested Michael for the job. He had accepted and taken over the branch which was down to less than fifty members.

Michael Williams's first move on taking over was to set up effective groups in all the surrounding villages. 'We've roughly doubled the number of auxiliaries, awful word that it is. Now we've got representatives in even the smallest hamlets.' The results, in terms both of membership and fund-raising, have been remarkable. Branch membership has quadrupled to over 400. In 1973 the village of Downderry, with less than 1,000 people, raised nearly £300 from its annual bring-and-buy sale. Boscastle, a romantic but tiny huddle of fishermen's cottages with a population of 500, raised £137 on the flag day: one person in every ten of the whole population helped collect the money.

Among other means of fund-raising Williams has also hit on the appropriate idea of sponsored walks by dogs. In collaboration with the fund for Guide Dogs for the Blind, one recent dog walk raised over £200, which was split between the two charities. In 1972 Williams handled 4,000 letters and phone calls. Few days go by without a talk to the local Inspector, David Locke, whose *rapport* with the branch is so good that he dropped the rank of Chief Inspector to come here. (Significantly, East Cornwall was the only branch I struck where the Inspector and branch secretary were on first-name terms. When I mentioned the point to Michael Williams he grinned and said it was probably against some Society by-law or other.)

Because of his journalistic connections Michael Williams has been able to get what he reckons is £1,000 worth of free advertising a year simply by telling local television stations and the press about interesting animal stories in the district. One event covered by Westward Television cameras was an open-air service at the village of Trevalga, which was attended by 200 humans and 150 animals and birds, ranging from horses to ferrets. Some people thought the idea sentimental, but Williams disagrees. 'I think it showed a lot of people the dignity of animals. As Lord Dowding said, "we're all on the ladder of evolution. We humans happen to be a few rungs higher."'

But the central problem in almost any branch is that of unwanted cats and dogs. Since Williams has been branch secretary, over 400 dogs have been found homes for, compared with what used to be a handful. A new unit of twelve kennels has been built for the Society's use in some local boarding kennels at Liskeard, helped by a grant from Headquarters of just on £3,000. It is fair to point out that rural Cornwall can hardly be compared with Liverpool – all the same it is typical of Michael Williams's attitude that since he took over no dog, unless it was sick or unmanageable, has been put down. 'The day we start putting down dogs', he says firmly, 'we find a new branch secretary.'

Besides the universal one of unwanted animals, I asked, does the branch have problems which are special to the region? Michael Williams said that because of its being such a remote area, the question of sub-standard breeding kennels was one the branch had been very much concerned with. Until 1974 the anomaly of the law had been that whereas boarding kennels and riding stables had to be licensed, breeding kennels did not.

Around 1970 the Inspector then stationed in the area had done a great deal of work in drawing attention to the existence of such kennels in East Cornwall. 'What he found', says Williams, 'was that there were some of these places where dogs were living in filthy conditions, often so underfed that prospective buyers would take them out of pity.' At one prosecution initiated by the Society, the kennel proprietor was fined £50, and a local solicitor described the kennels as a canine chamber of horrors.

Partly as a result of this local initiative, the RSPCA set up a national survey of conditions in breeding kennels, and in 1972 Michael Williams put up a motion to the Society's annual general meeting. All this helped to prepare the way for the Bill successfully introduced, in April 1973, by Gordon Oakes, Labour M.P. for Widnes, which finally established that breeding kennels should be subject to licensing and regular inspection.

Williams's view of how a branch should be effectively run is that it ultimately depends on the ordinary members. 'It's important to have people who can be seen doing something practical, as opposed to simply rattling a tin on flag days. Of course the practical work depends primarily on the Inspector – if someone reports a cat up a tree or a donkey down a tin mine, it's a job for him. But that doesn't mean branch members are only good for having coffee mornings.'

One of the things ordinary branch members can do, Michael Williams believes, is to help find homes for unwanted animals. Beyond this, most branches will always have a few people capable of actually handling animals in distress and thus reducing the Inspector's load of work. One Tintagel couple, Aubrey and Maureen Edwards, have already turned the field at the back of their house into a sanctuary for injured seabirds. Some of the birds are brought in by the Inspector, others from people in the village who have got to know that the Edwards family will take in injured birds.

'If one of the kids at school finds a damaged seabird,' says Maureen Edwards, 'my children'll pipe up and say, bring it to our mum.'

Apart from having been trained as a nurse, Maureen Edwards had no particular qualifications when she started the work. 'At first',

97

she says, 'I knew so little about birds that I had to look them up in a book, to see what was their natural habitat and food.' Now, partly as the result of her nursing training, she has learned to make tiny splints from emery boards and Elastoplast. If she has a problem she cannot handle, she takes the seabird to the vet for treatment. When the birds are ready for release, they simply take off from the garage roof. 'They know better than we do when they're ready to go', she says. 'They get their bearings to the sea, then take off. Of course we get fond of them, but I love to see them go. Off to the wild remoteness of the oceans.'

*

Another way in which the branches can usefully link to the main organization is in running pilot schemes for special campaigns. When the Council decided in 1972 to mount a campaign on the sterilizing of domestic pets, one of the branches approached was Windsor, which had recently become considerably revitalized through the efforts of a dynamic ex-Naval commander named Innes Hamilton, now an investment consultant in the city. In the course of three years, Hamilton had brought the Windsor membership from five to over 1,000. All the same, nobody had yet thought out the problems involved in mounting a large publicity exercise on this scale. It was just the sort of challenge for which the Windsor branch had been waiting.

Innes Hamilton sat down with his committee, then started talking to the local vets. 'The first object', he says, 'was to get the public to bring in their own animals. The second was to provide money and transport to help the elderly and less well off. If necessary, we were going to have to take their animals to the vets for them.'

Initially the branch placed a series of advertisements in all local papers urging people to take cats to their own vet to have them spayed. For people who did not have a regular vet of their own, a list of all local practices was included. The advertisement also stressed the environmental aspect: Hamilton makes the point that if the Society was not there to organize something like it, local government would have to. 'Stray dogs not only foul the street, they're a potential cause of road accidents as well.'

By the autumn of 1972 the Windsor campaign was firmly under way. The branch got a special telephone line installed, so that people could ring up for the names of vets, or if necessary for practical assistance in getting their animals to them. To help with this, Hamilton recruited a team of volunteer girl drivers called Waves – Windsor Animal Volunteer Emergency Service. If an old-age pensioner wants her cat spayed, the Wave will fix the appointment with the vet, and physically transport the animal there and back to the operation. 'As long as the cat's not up a tree on the morning of the appointment,' says Hamilton, 'the arrangement's fairly foolproof. The Wave reassures the old lady, brings the animal home, and then takes it back to have the stitches out the following week.' In cases of need the Society will also bear the cost, which is around £2 for male cats and £4 for females. The result of the pilot scheme is that after a year, over 4,500 cat have been spayed at an average cost to the Society of 70p. The point is not simply the total, but the fact that Windsor has been able to establish guidelines for a nationwide campaign.

Another way in which the branches keep in touch is through the sixteen Regional Organizers: Peter Pine-Coffin, who takes in seven branches and 304 auxiliaries in the North Midlands, told me he sees the job as being a sort of ambassador for Headquarters. 'Pushing their policies down to the grass roots, and hoping the grass roots will like them. I'm here to see the branches are as active as they can be, and that everyone works as a team. At the same time, I've got no power over them. I can try to persuade them to do something that seems for the good of the Society. But if they don't want to, I can't force them.'

I asked how many of his seven branches were what he would call really active. Peter Pine-Coffin said he thought they were all pretty active now, but that it had been very easy for a branch to get run down, so it became ineffective. 'When I came here there was one branch where they hadn't kept the minutes for thirty years. The branch in question had £9,000 in the bank, no animal home, and was virtually held together by the energy of three auxiliary secretaries. I took my life in my hands and called a committee meeting. I told them unless they were prepared to reorganize things there was nothing I could do to help.' In the end the committee had been re-formed, and one of the auxiliary secretaries had taken over the main branch. After a year it had become a flourishing concern. Even so, he said, it had taken a lot of work on the part of the members.

Ultimately, enthusiasm is the quality that matters in the branches. One example in Peter Pine-Coffin's own area is the Derby branch, which till recently had eighty members and an animal home which had become run down. Now the branch has been taken over and revitalized, largely through the branch secretary, Jill Davies, who, besides being a housewife and mother, is a trained nurse and

99

freelance journalist. In two years the membership has risen to 300, the dogs' home has been cleaned up, and the branch is actively engaged on fund-raising to buy premises for a new one.

The Human Face

Any charity must ultimately depend on how the public sees it. The man chiefly responsible for how the public sees the RSPCA is a highly successful advertising man named Mike Seymour-Rouse. A tough, ebullient Cornishman with a look of Kenneth More, he has been Publicity & Appeals Officer since 1970.

Even in the short time he has been there he has seen a considerable change of emphasis in the Society's work. 'I think that up till a few years ago the Society was putting pretty well all its effort into helping domestic animals. We were in danger of becoming a cat and dog society – we were failing to realize that it's just as cruel to crowd chickens into batteries as to put spurs on cockerels and let them fight to the death. What we've come to realize over the last ten years is that cruelty has a million faces.'

Recognizing the modern faces of cruelty is very much more than a job to Mike Seymour-Rouse. When I went to see him at his cottage at St. Margaret's Bay, a tiny clutch of houses nestling under Dover Cliffs, he told me something of his background. He had always had a feeling for animals, he said: one of the first things that had been impressed on his memory was a verse from Coleridge written up in the dining hall at school:

He prayeth best, who loveth best
All things both great and small,
For the dear God who loveth us,
He made and loveth all.

The lines had made a profound impression – but the feeling for animals had not been all. During the war Mike was captured at Dunkirk, and made four escapes from prison camps in Germany. Once he and another officer escaped together, dressed as a German farm labourer and his wife. 'Unfortunately we got picked up trying to buy a ticket at the local railway station', he recalls. 'But that was only the third time. After my next escape, I was sent to Dachau for interrogation.'

What he saw in one of the grimmest of all the concentration camps impressed him with a feeling that somewhere along the line he wanted to do something to increase the sum of human kindness. It is very powerfully, you feel, what motivates him still. He came home from the war, joined a large American advertising agency in which he rose to be International Director. Then, in 1970, he found the kind of opportunity he had always been looking for with the RSPCA. 'In one sense animal welfare's only part of it', he says. 'The way a child treats an animal will very often be the way he treats people weaker than himself in later life. In the Society's rules, it says that one of our main aims is the promotion of kindness. That's what I believe the Society is all about.'

How did he feel, though, I asked, about the image that a lot of people still have of the RSPCA as being rather extensively composed of sentimental old ladies?

Mike said he thought it was important to distinguish between sentimentality and sentiment. 'If someone substitutes an animal for a human as an object of love, that's sad. At the same time you've got to remember that loneliness is one of the afflictions of today's society. An animal can be the linch-pin of an old-age pensioner's existence – the only living creature that doesn't regard them as old and useless and on the shelf.'

We strolled down to the Coastguard pub at the other end of the beach. Sitting on the wall with the seagulls wheeling against the blue sky, it seemed a long way from the world of cruelty.

'I don't think you ever do escape the world of cruelty, though', said Mike. 'You've only got to take those seagulls. If they get their wings oiled, it's because you and I insist on having motor-cars which need oil brought through the Channel. In an affluent society you get what I call the sophisticated cruelties. More and more people getting a taste for white veal, which for the sake of a little culinary snobbery means the calf suffering horribly.' The previous week there had been a seal-cull in the Wash: hundreds of baby seals had been killed allegedly because of the damage they do to the fishing harvest. 'It could have been in the interests of fishing to shoot the old ones, but not the baby seals. They got killed because you get £15 a pelt – there's a big market for sealskin coats, not to keep people warm, but as a status symbol.'

How did the actual publicity and fund-raising work? Mike said that it was a pretty important sphere of the Society's work and always had been. One of the first recorded minutes reported Arthur Broome's getting a prominent vicar to preach a sermon against cruelty.

Modern publicity methods stress specific themes. This poster was part of a campaign on factory farming. *Opposite*, 'They're as much concern to us as anyone'. This advertisement aimed to show concern for animals as part of a wider compassion.

Nowadays the public relations may still include a sermon: a favourite event of Mike's is the March of Concern to Westminster Abbey every Christmas. 'This is an example', he says, 'of how one charity can help another. On the March of Concern a thousand children, collecting for the Save the Children Fund, walk with a crib of live animals to the Abbey.'

Some of his other projects had at first caused a few raised eyebrows, he admitted with a grin, such as the big campaign he had run in conjunction with a firm of petfood manufacturers. 'The point was that we brought our name before the public, and the net result for animals was very good, both in terms of money and publicity. As a result of that one campaign, we were able to help equip a new animal hospital.'

Working with other charities. The Christmas March
of Concern to Westminster Abbey is organized jointly with
the Save the Children Fund and the Salvation Army.

Was there a tendency, I asked, if you were working in the sophisticated world of advertising, to lose sight of the actual objective? When
he was working on a major publicity campaign, did he ever imagine a
suffering animal at the end of it?

Mike considered the question for a bit, then said he'd tell me a story.
Not long ago he had been with an Italian film crew at the Harmsworth
Animal Hospital in North London. They had been filming a vet doing
something with a cat, while the child who owned the cat sat watching.
The camera had been on the cat, then Mike suddenly noticed the
child's expression and nudged the director. The Italian had glowed
with joy, panned on to the child's face, and got one of the most moving
pictures Mike had ever seen of a child's concern for a pet.

'Does that answer the question? What I see at the end of the line is
a human face. It may be a child learning the ways of kindness. It may
be an old-age pensioner made happier because we could help out with
their vet's bill. In the end it all comes back to kindness.'

4 : The SELFA Story

'What is the point of a very thorough series of laws built up over the years to protect animals . . . if we then shut our eyes to the final 10 days which can involve stress, terror and finally a cruel death?'

RSPCA Statement of Intent on Live Food Animals

One evening in January 1973 the Chairman of the RSPCA, John Hobhouse, was just going to bed when the phone rang.

'John? It's Freddie here.' The caller was Frederick Burden, M.P. for Gillingham, and Vice-Chairman of the Society.

'I thought you'd like to be the first to know. The Ministry have clamped down on the export of live sheep to Europe. No further licences will be issued from midnight.'

For Hobhouse and the Society, the news meant the end of a three-year battle. Even so, it was not the end of the campaign. Because it had been the toughest, but most effective the Society has fought in recent years, it is worth looking at in a little detail.

*

As far back as the turn of the century there had been the problem of cruelty to animals exported to the continent. Earlier in this book, you remember, we looked at the sufferings of the run-down British cab horses which were shipped to Antwerp to end their days in Belgian slaughter-houses. Gradually over the years, the brutal trade in horses had been stopped. Then, after the second World War, there had been a new development. This time the trade was in sheep and cattle.

There were two basic reasons why this trade developed. The first was the shortage of meat, especially beef, for American servicemen stationed in post-war Europe. The second was that in those days British slaughter-houses, though invariably more humane, did not have the standards of inspection enforced by State Department standards. The American servicemen wanted British beef, but preferred it killed in Europe.

'There's a big market for sealskin coats. Not to keep people warm but as a status symbol'.

Thus a trade in live food animals had slowly developed through the 1950s. It was an arrangement that suited many British exporters, who could earn a high price for their sheep and cattle. It also suited the continental buyers, for it provided good business for their slaughter-houses. Because the animals were killed in their own yards, it also meant that they were buying not only carcasses, but also the valuable by-products of hides and offal.

But what about the conditions for the animals themselves? Through the 1950s, the RSPCA had been unhappily aware that many animals were travelling in conditions of stress. On humane grounds, the Society would by far have preferred a carcass trade in which the animals would have been humanely slaughtered in British yards, then exported as dead meat. Largely as a result of the Society's recommendations, a special sub-committee of the Board of Trade was set up under Lord Balfour to explore the whole question in 1957.

The committee produced four main recommendations which have since been regarded as the guidelines for the conditions under which live animals should travel. Very simply, the Balfour Assurances as they became known, were these. Firstly, no animal should travel more than 100 kilometres from the port of disembarkation – for example Antwerp or Ostend – to the place where they were to be slaughtered. Secondly, they were to be adequately fed and watered during their journey. Thirdly, when they did reach the slaughter-house, they were to be humanely killed either by electric pre-stunning, or by the captive-bolt pistol method, long in use in the United Kingdom.

Fourthly – and it was this condition which was later to lead to some of the more cloak-and-dagger adventures of the RSPCA investigating teams – no animal sent from Britain to one continental country could be re-exported to another. In other words, cattle or sheep travelling to Belgium had to be slaughtered in Belgium – they could not be taken across the frontier and slaughtered in France. These, very simply, were the Assurances agreed between Britain, Belgium, Holland, West Germany, and later Italy. France – and this point was to be highly relevant later – was committed for cattle only. This meant that no sheep could be legally exported for slaughtering in France.

Ideally the Society would still have preferred a carcass trade. In the meantime the Balfour Assurances seemed as good as anything it was likely to get. As long as they were actually observed, it seemed that British animals would be to a considerable extent protected.

At this point there enters one of the principal actors in the story: an RSPCA Inspector named Ronald Butfield, who in 1960 had been transferred to the Medway Towns in Kent. It was a singularly suitable appointment. The Medway Towns make up one of the tougher patches for an Inspector, comprising a mixture of docks, and urban as well as rural areas. Butfield was energetic, quick-witted, and with a commitment to animal welfare that went far beyond the line of duty. During the war he had been involved in special operations in the Adriatic, where one of his main jobs had been to assist the escape of British airmen who had been sheltered by Tito's partisans. Now, arriving at Medway, he found that his expertise with boats was likely to come in useful. One of the places in his area was the port of Sheerness. And Sheerness was one of the main centres for the export of live food animals to Europe.

By the time Butfield took up his duties, the export trade was booming. So many animals were arriving daily that huge new pens or lairages, as they are technically known, were spreading across the Sheerness dockyard. Butfield began to spend more and more time at the docks, getting to know the Spanish and Portuguese crews who manned the cattle boats. Most days he watched the conditions under which the animals were travelling, and sometimes he gave a hand with them. 'My view', he recalls, 'was that however much I might dislike it personally, it was a perfectly legal trade. My job as an Inspector was to see that it was done humanely.'

There was no apparent cruelty at the Sheerness end. What disturbed Butfield, though, were chance remarks from the crews about what went on on the other side of the Channel. One day a Spanish sailor told Butfield that it seemed odd that they weren't allowed to beat the cattle with sticks at Sheerness, when Belgian dockyard workers were often beating the living daylights out of them at Ostend.

Butfield decided to take a couple of trips across the Channel himself – the first time by agreement with the exporters, and the second time unofficially without their knowledge. 'When I went over with the exporter's permission, everything was properly done. Then I got a Dutch skipper to take me over on the quiet. This time I saw the cattle being pushed and shoved all over Ostend Docks. The crews were using bits of stick, with lengths of fire-hose tied to them.'

Thus Butfield's suspicions had been aroused in the mid-1960s. Meanwhile there was no evidence that the Balfour rules were being consistently broken. At this point we must briefly pause and look at something else which was to become highly relevant to the story.

*

Over the Society's long history, one of its most important functions has always been the encouragement of humane legislation. In the earliest days, indeed, it had virtually grown up as the means of enforcing Martin's law. Then, as time went on, the Society had gone on to promote the kind of legislation it knew to be necessary. Such landmarks as Pease's Bill to protect domestic animals in 1835 and the all-embracing Animals' Act of 1911 have already been mentioned. Sometimes the Acts of Parliament had been the work of M.P.s who were also members of the Society's Council. Another extremely useful ally in the post-war years had been the small all-party committee known as the Parliamentary Animal Welfare Group. Though in no way officially connected with the Society, the Group had been an effective instrument in promoting legislation. Often it would do this in close collaboration with the Society's Parliamentary Liaison Officer whose job it is to see that M.P.s are provided with all information likely to be of help.

This useful and productive state of affairs had long continued. Then, almost out of the blue, something happened to change it. The Annual General Meeting in 1969 had carried a motion that the Society should spend a certain amount of its funds on publicity which might lead to an eventual ban on hare-coursing. It had never occurred to anyone in the Society that this might be an improper use of funds. All the same, the decision was challenged by a group of members of the British Field Sports Society. As a charitable body, they said, the Society could not use its funds to try to bring about changes in the law. If it attempted to do so, the group threatened, they would challenge its charitable status. This would mean that the Society would no longer qualify for the tax exemption allowed to charities.

Faced with the possibility of a large loss of income, the Society sought legal advice to clarify the position. Technically, they were told, their challengers were in the right. As a charity, the Society could not use its funds to seek changes in the law. Although in the view of some members, the Society's acquiescence was a little timid, the Council decided it could not risk serious financial loss.

Since 1969, therefore, it has had to walk a narrow legal tightrope. 'What we can't do,' says the Executive Director, Major Ronald Seager, 'is to go to an M.P. and suggest that he brings in a Bill we should like to see enacted. On the other hand, once a Member has put forward a Bill of his own, we can put our views to him and other members. And we can go to a Minister or permanent official with facts which make the need for legislation obvious.'

In the coming battle for the live food animals, there were soon to be plenty of such facts. The obvious legislation, though, was to be a long time coming.

*

Meanwhile at RSPCA Headquarters in 1970, various changes were taking place. Ronald Butfield had been appointed to the top job in the Inspectorate, that of Chief Superintendent. At the same time the Society had also appointed a new chief vet, Philip Brown, who was known as an expert on farm animals. Now, for the first time, Butfield felt something might be done about the trade he had wanted to stop since his Sheerness days. 'As soon as I met Philip Brown', he recalls, 'I realized that here was someone who would carry weight. I thought, if we could present the Ministry with a report based on his specialist knowledge and my experience of investigations, then they'd have to listen.'

On 20 October 1970 Brown and Butfield set off on what was to be the first of many visits to Ostend. Introducing themselves to the foreign buyers as a British vet and a colleague interested in the transportation of livestock, they met with a cautious but guarded welcome. They were shown slaughter-houses where conditions seemed to be humane – all the same Butfield noted there was clear evidence that animals were being re-exported across the border. Until 25 October nothing had really happened which seemed to justify their journey.

But on that day something did happen, and it was the point from which everything else in the story flows. Arriving back at Ostend from Holland, the two men heard that a load of barley-fed calves was due that evening at Zeebrugge. Following a hunch, they decided to wait to see the calves arriving at the Ostend lairage.

As soon as he saw the calves, Brown noticed something. He recognized them as white veal-calves, which had been fed on milk. Technically it was not a point covered by the Balfour rules, but it occurred to Brown that the importer was evading certain regulations. If the calves were barley-fed, they would be subject to an import duty of 16 per cent. If they were milk-fed, the tax would be exactly double. Thus if the importers were breaking one rule, they might well be breaking others. If he could see the calves after they had actually been slaughtered, Brown could definitely establish the point about milk-feeding. He went over to the British exporter's area manager on the quay and asked where the animals would be going for slaughter.

110

The SELFA poster.

To Brown's surprise the manager, whom he remembers as a like-able young man, not only told him the name of the slaughter-house, but added that he would be glad if Brown would have a look at it: he had seen something of the conditions there, he said, and had not liked them. The slaughter-house itself was at a place called Putté, 180 kilometres from Zeebrugge. Thus the first of the Balfour rules – the one governing the distance animals were allowed to travel – was clearly being broken.

By now the suspicions of both men were thoroughly aroused. They asked the English exporter to telephone the Putté abattoir to say they would like to see the calves both before and after slaughter. The abattoir owner agreed and told them to be there at 11.30 in the morning. Brown and Butfield decided to take no chances. Next morning they drove up to the Putté slaughter-house two hours before the time they had been told. Even so, they were only just in time. As they drove in, the lorry which had brought the animals from Zeebrugge was already leaving. Clearly they had not been intended to see the actual slaughtering taking place, and in view of what they now saw, it hardly seemed surprising. Philip Brown's report takes up the story:

Philip Brown, the Society's chief vet, played a leading role in the SELFA campaign.

Slaughtering methods and the slaughter-house itself can only be described as barbaric. The method of stunning used was to hit the animal over the head with an ordinary carpenter's claw hammer. I found no bullet holes, but in one or two cases fractured frontal bones. The calves may, or may not, have been stunned by this method. The calf was then hoisted by the hind leg by a travelling hoist and its throat was cut. Out of deference to us, the slaughterman was requested by the manager to use a Cash pistol while we were there, but he resented having to use it and was not proficient in its use. The pistol had not been greased for some time and was not working satisfactorily.

Demonstrators at the House of Commons.

The calves were crowded into a killing pen about 6 feet by 12 feet, one end of which was the bleeding area. When a calf had been stunned it was shackled to the hoist and dragged through other living calves which were sometimes actually thrown into the blood bath by the unconscious calf on its way up the hoist. There was only a galvanized pipe preventing the live calves going into the rest of the slaughter-house and these calves were all killed within sight of each other, and also could see only 2 feet from them, their fellows' throats cut and could see the pile of decapitated heads in one corner.

What had now been established beyond doubt, was that the Balfour rules were being broken.

*

But what in fact could the Society do? Because of the sensitive relationship with Parliament, there seemed little hope of a Private Member's Bill which might legislate against the traffic. True, the Society could put the facts to the Ministry of Agriculture. But at that particular time the Heath Government was itself treading the delicate path towards entry into Europe. Anxious at all costs to avoid difficulties with its Common Market neighbours, it maintained the view that the Balfour rules were still an adequate safeguard. (In fairness, it must be said that the Government did make representations to Belgium about the Putté slaughter-house, as a result of which no more British cattle were sent there. But in a sense the point only goes to show that Putté was seen officially as an isolated instance.)

Meanwhile support for the Society's protest was beginning to spread across the country. Philip Brown, on his return from Belgium, had written a letter about the Putté conditions to the *Veterinary Record*. It had been published, along with a strong editorial comment entirely supporting the RSPCA investigations. The press conference given by Brown and Butfield after their return had also attracted wide publicity.

All this might help, but it was not enough. If the Government was to be persuaded of the need for action, more evidence was clearly needed. Between the end of 1970 and the autumn of 1971, the Society's officials made many more trips to Europe.

Much of the time was spent on sheer boring inactivity. Because all evidence had to be meticulous and foolproof, Butfield used often to spend all night watching a lorry-load of sheep so that nobody could say they had been fed and watered while he wasn't looking. 'For one hour of activity there were often twenty-three where nothing happened', he recalls. At other times he would find himself pursuing lorries for hundreds of miles down French roads, driving till he was so tired he began to see two lorries. 'The trouble was that the lorry drivers would get a meal or a sleep, but we couldn't. If he went into a house he might be going for a meal or a sleep or to see his girl friend. We had to stay outside, because once we'd lost him, we'd lost him for good.'

Slowly but surely this systematic observation began to pay off. At Sisteron in Provence, Philip Brown saw 420 English sheep being slaughtered by having their throats cut, while an abattoir worker held them on their backs to keep them still. Another team followed a load of sheep to Marseilles, twelve times the distance allowed by the Balfour Committee. At no stage on the journey were they either fed or watered. Among the drivers and slaughtermen such conditions were taken for granted. 'Their view was that the animals were going to die anyway', says Butfield. 'So in their view, what did it matter?'

*

It was two years since the question of the live food animals had first been raised in Whitehall. Now, through the summer and autumn of 1972, a series of deputations from the Society received a series of dusty answers. Faced with the now obvious breakdown of the Balfour rules, the Ministry began to shift its ground.

No longer relying on the Balfour rules, they now said that the best control would be the implementation of a Council of Europe plan for livestock transportation. Drawn up ten years previously, the plan had still not been ratified. Nevertheless, the Ministry would be prepared to trust it. The Society's answer to this scheme was categoric. In the absence of any continental system of inspection comparable to the RSPCA's, said John Hobhouse, there was no possibility of enforcing such a system. Another time Brown went with a deputation to see the Under-Secretary, Miss Peggy Fenner. 'She asked whether we had any more up-to-date information of the rules being broken. I said, how up-to-date do you want it – would yesterday do?' As it happened, Brown had come back from the continent the previous day, when he had actually seen sheep being taken across the Belgian frontier.

Meanwhile John Hobhouse and the RSPCA Council, faced with the realization that they were making no headway in Whitehall, had come to a decision. What was needed was a major campaign to appeal to public opinion. By a stroke of luck this had been made possible despite the problem over charitable status. Each November in Parliament there is a ballot for Private Members' Bills, and among the successful M.P.s in November 1972 had been Sir Ronald Russell, a member of the Society's Council. He had immediately presented a Bill to control the export of live food animals to Europe. The Bill had made no progress, but the point was that it was before the House. The Society, without risking its charitable status, could now seek to influence public opinion.

That winter the Society swung into action with the biggest campaign the Publicity Department had ever mounted. Based on the slogan SELFA – *Stop the Export of Live Food Animals* – its basic symbol was the brilliantly effective one of a cow and a sheep in the cut-away hold of a ship, heaving at an angle on a rolling sea. The blue and orange symbol was distributed nationally in the form of children's badges, car stickers and even signs in butchers' shops.

By the slogan 'Does Your M.P. Know the Facts?', sympathizers were invited – as they now could be since Sir Ronald Russell's Bill was before the Commons – to urge their M.P.s to vote for the abolition of the trade. Apart from the humane factor, the publicity adroitly pointed out, Britain was also losing money by it. Not only were some of our own slaughter-houses working at less than half their capacity, but the country was having to import large quantities of meat – much of it to replace the animals exported.

As Christmas 1972 approached, it began to look as if things were moving. (Chief Superintendent Butfield, it might be added, was in France right up to Christmas Eve. With the kind of ingenuity he and Brown had now learned from experience, they decided it would be worth watching the ports at Christmas, when no one would be likely to expect them.)

Meanwhile at Headquarters the finishing touches were being put to a new project. This, as things turned out, would be decisive.

*

For several weeks before Christmas, confidential discussions had been going on between the Society's Publicity Department and the BBC. The idea was that the *Midweek* programme should carry a feature on the export of live food animals. The BBC would pay the cost – what they wanted from the Society was the co-operation and experience of a trained investigator. On 16 January 1973 Butfield went over to Ostend for a preliminary reconnaissance with one of the *Midweek* producers.

The SELFA exhibition train toured main provincial
centres and was seen by 25,000 people.

On the 21st the rest of the BBC camera team arrived in Ostend. As
on Brown and Butfield's original trip, for the first day or so nothing
happened. Butfield saw several lorry-loads of sheep which he had
reason to suppose were going to be taken through France to North
Africa or Greece, but there was one difficulty. Since the RSPCA had
begun their investigations, the exporters had developed considerable
ingenuity to avoid them. One device was to mix lorry-loads of English
animals with others which had been brought from Ireland. Obviously
the cruelty was just as great   but Ireland had never been a signatory to
the Balfour Assurances. If Butfield and the BBC team followed what
turned out to be a load of Irish sheep, they might find evidence of
cruelty, but it would cut no ice in Whitehall.

On the afternoon of 25 January there began to be signs of much more
activity in Ostend Docks. At one point there were five French lorries
loading sheep, all indisputably English. Following Butfield's hunch,

the BBC team tagged along behind two of these lorries to Steenevorde, on the French frontier.

When they arrived at Steenevorde, the lorries were at once joined by five others containing English sheep, all arriving from Belgium.

By this time Butfield knew they were on to a major consignment. His suspicion was intensified when a man he recognized as a major French importer arrived at the frontier post while the BBC were filming. 'Things were made more difficult', recalls Butfield, 'by the arrival of the French police. They insisted on confiscating the film the camera team had been shooting, then arresting us.' Eventually Butfield and the camera team were released, but only on condition they surrendered the film. 'We made a great show of indignation, kicking the lorry tyres and swearing. As soon as they'd moved off we nipped back across the frontier and dug up the real film which we had buried by a café.'

What followed was possibly the most decisive forty-eight hours in the SELFA story and certainly the most exciting. All through the night of the 25th, Butfield and the camera team pursued the lorries, despite the drivers' attempts to shake them off. 'They used every device they knew', says Butfield. 'They'd move into the fast lane, then try swinging off into a by-lane. After two years following French lorries, we were used to this.'

Towards midnight on the 25th the lorries pulled off the road at a garage, and once more the camera crew began filming. This time there was an argument between the importer, the driver, and the BBC team. In the end one BBC man was chased off by the driver, brandishing one of the tools from his lorry.

Twenty minutes later, the team resumed pursuit. Soon after midnight one of the two lorries turned off the motorway. Following Butfield's hunch, the team followed the other. By five o'clock on the morning of the 26th, they had driven 440 kilometres from the frontier. Butfield's report takes up the story:

At this stage the weather was bitterly cold, below freezing, with a very heavy ground frost and the trees outlined with frost and ice . . . At 0725 hours the driver proceeded without making a check of the sheep . . .

At 0823 hours he stopped 536 kilometres from Steenevorde and cleaned the ice from his driving windows . . . At 0835 hours he proceeded again, and the signpost read that it was 200 kilometres further on to Lyons. By this time there was fog, the frost was very thick and I managed to check the sheep during the stop. I found several down on their sides. They were extremely tired, they were hungry and distressed and the outside ones had frost on their coats . . . There was no bedding whatsoever and certainly no feed for them.

Meanwhile the BBC crew had been filming continuously. At 11 o'clock on the morning of the 26th the lorries passed the toll point at Lyons. The sheep had now travelled 717 kilometres from Steenevorde. At midday the lorry left the Lyons motorway to turn east for Grenoble. Butfield's report goes on:

At 1530 hours we were *en route* through the French Alps, on mountain roads . . . at 1545 hours the lorry stopped on a mountain bend to let a coach pass. It was unable to continue because the transmission shaft had broken. The weather was bitterly cold and the temperature was below freezing. The traffic was held up and a check of the sheep revealed that they were miserable and distressed, pawing the decks for food, sucking at pieces of chain or rope outside the vehicle for what moisture they could get . . . Several of the sheep were down, some on their sides. It was impossible to enter the vehicle because of the customs seals and I could only get a few of the sheep up from the outside and hope that the remainder were not suffocated . . .

The following morning at 0830 hours, 27th January, 1973, I again observed the sheep. It had snowed heavily throughout the night, the temperature was sub-zero and there was a light blizzard blowing with slight fog . . . The increase in the number of sheep coughing indicated distress. There was no evidence in the snow that there had been any inspection of the vehicle at all throughout the night . . . There was no food or water in evidence.

The rest of the story can be briefly told. Next day the sheep arrived at the slaughter-house at Sisteron. No filming was allowed once they arrived there – not surprisingly perhaps, since this was the slaughter-house where, a year before, RSPCA investigators had seen animals being held down while having their throats cut. By the time the sheep arrived there, they had travelled two and a half days, much of the time in blizzard conditions, with neither food nor water. As for Butfield, he had been arrested three times in less than as many days. In the end, because his association with the RSPCA would have led to the film's being confiscated, he had to pose as the BBC team's driver.

Thanks to the *Midweek* team and the RSPCA, the Sisteron sheep were among the last, possibly the very last, to suffer such conditions.

On the night of 31 January the Minister of Agriculture, the Rt. Hon. Joseph Godber, told the House of Commons that no more export licences would be issued for live sheep to go to Europe.

Perhaps the Minister's decision was not unconnected with the fact that the BBC film was due to be shown the following night. Or perhaps, as one M.P. said later, he had, like Paul on the road to Damascus, been suddenly converted.

Whatever the reason, the Society had won a major battle. But they had not yet won the whole campaign, for the ban still did not apply to cattle.

*

Letters from constituents were now pouring into M.P.s' postbags. The film attracted widespread feeling and the question of the live food animals was becoming a matter of concern to Members of all parties, and not only those active in animal welfare. In the Commons Sir Ronald Russell's Bill, blocked by the farming lobby, had failed its Second Reading. Another RSPCA Council member, Frederick Burden, had put down an Early Day Motion calling for the ban to be extended to cattle as well as sheep. It had been signed by more than 160 Members, but the point about an Early Day Motion is that it can only be debated if time is allowed by the Leader of the House. Having given way over the sheep, the Government was not anxious to do the same for cattle.

'The decision to suspend export licences for sheep', said Earl Ferrers, the Government spokesman on agriculture in the Lords, 'was taken as a result of widespread breaches of the Balfour Assurances. There have been no comparable substantiated reports which would justify similar action in respect of cattle.'

The Society, it seemed, was back to square one. Almost all the effort of the last two years had been concentrated on sheep. Now, they had to find a whole new mass of evidence on cattle, and another problem was that the exporters were stepping up their attempt to confuse the investigating teams by mixing Irish cattle with English. To prove that the Balfour rules were being broken, the Society would need to show that the cattle had not simply been travelling through Britain *en route* from Ireland. They would, for instance, need to have seen the Ministry's official subsidy mark, a small punched hole in the ear of an animal in question.

The export of live animals to Europe. These *News of the World* photographs helped to bring the facts before the British public. In the second photo (*overleaf*) note the bullock being prodded, while in the third photo animals arriving at the slaughter-house are being driven past those already killed.

Through the first few months of 1973 the Society's campaign to win over public opinion had been gaining mass support. In February a SELFA train, carrying pictures, facts and irrefutable statistics had begun to tour the country. Visiting every major population centre, it had been seen by 25,000 people. As a result, support began to flow in from such bodies as universities, townswomen's guilds, city and rural councils. Help came from Society members, particularly Mrs. A. M. Allen, who had concerned herself with the export trade right from the early days. 'Mrs. Allen's help was invaluable', says Ronald Butfield. 'She was on the phone to the Ministry day after day, literally bombarding them with facts and giving them no quarter.'

The National Union of Agricultural Workers pledged their support and so did the meat and refrigeration trades. In Plymouth, SELFA bookmarks were stuck in 2,000 books at the public library. At Rotherham in Yorkshire, an ice-cream man distributed the literature on his daily rounds. Such opposition as there was came from the National Farmers' Union, which had sent its own delegation to Holland. 'Of course there was some good-humoured shouting and slapping on the rump', said their report. 'It was no different from normal practice in slaughter-houses in England.'

Good-humoured slapping on the rump might not entirely accord with Brown and Butfield's findings. Certainly it was not confirmed by a story which appeared in the *News of the World* on 18 March, describing conditions in the Izegem abattoir in Belgium. Written by Maureen Lawless, a 22-year-old freelance reporter from Birmingham, the report made the grimmest reading yet put before the British public. The terrified animals, she said:

were beaten into the concrete killing area where a man with a pistol aimed haphazardly at them as they were pushed past him.

Some animals fell shot in the head. Others not so fortunate were shot in the ear, the cheek or the top of the neck.

The cattle behind them fell over the dead and injured bodies into the blood which was inches deep.

One injured beast somehow crawled away and wedged itself under some bars in the corner.

As shot animals were falling down or trying to stagger away, they were hauled up by a chain attached to one hind leg and were left to have their throats cut in full view of the other beasts.

One steer with a wound in its cheek was hanging up by one leg kicking and struggling and bellowing for minutes fully conscious before one of the men walked over and actually cut its throat.

By this time it was almost impossible to distinguish the live from the dead animals.

*

There was one other point not mentioned in the report. One of the pictures taken by the *News of the World* photographer showed quite clearly a small punched hole in the ear of one of the cattle. It was the Ministry's official subsidy mark, which proved beyond doubt that these were English cattle.

Even so, the SELFA campaign was not quite won. For the next three months more and more school-children continued to display the blue and orange badges, and more backing came from public bodies. By May more than a million car stickers, bookmarks, and posters had been sent out. On 21 June 1973 there came the most authoritative support so far, when the British Veterinary Association announced itself in favour of a carcass-only trade, and condemned all long journeys to slaughter-houses. Such backing was not, especially since the *Veterinary Record*'s leader on the Putté conditions, entirely unexpected. But the next step in the SELFA story was something that nobody, certainly nobody in the RSPCA, had ever dreamed of.

One of the time-honoured processes of Parliamentary procedure is what are known as Supply Days. The Opposition has twenty-eight of these days in each session. On a Supply Day, they may bring up any matter which they urgently wish debated. Normally animal welfare is a subject which Parliament might regard as suitable material for a Private Member's Bill, but hardly for a Supply Day Motion.

But on this subject of the export of live animals, the Labour Opposition knew, there was widespread feeling throughout the country – and on 11 July they had a Supply Day. When the Shadow Cabinet met in the first week of July to decide what motions to put forward on the 11th they decided on two. One was a motion to discuss the shortage of police manpower. The other, put down in the names of Harold Wilson and Edward Short, the Deputy Leader, was a motion to suspend all licences for the export of live food animals.

To be realistic, it must be added that the Opposition knew there was at least a handful of Conservative Members who, despite a three-line whip, would vote against their party: more than sixty Conservatives, in fact, had signed Frederick Burden's motion. The result was by no means certain, but it was conceivable that a full-scale debate might mean defeat for the Conservative administration. On the other hand it would be deeply unjust to the traditional idealism of the Labour Party to imply this as a major reason. 'Of course we knew there might be political mileage in it for us', one Labour M.P. told me, 'but it wasn't what motivated us. If a Tory backbencher had put up the same motion, I'd have voted for it.'

Meanwhile for Tory backbenchers like Frederick Burden, there could only be one answer to the dilemma of voting according to conscience, or a three-line whip. 'Of course nobody likes having to vote against their party', said Mr. Burden. 'But this is democracy. This is what we're here for.'

When it came to the division only 23 of the 65 Conservatives who had signed Burden's Early Day motion were prepared to defy the whip and vote with the Opposition, but it was enough. Defeated by 285 votes to 265, the Government next day announced a ban on all further exports.

At last the long campaign was over. One RSPCA man heard the result of the division from the Public Gallery. 'There were a lot of ghosts in the House that night', he said. 'I like to think one of them was Richard Martin's.'

In some ways the campaign had been fought with the most sophisti-cated weapons the Society had ever used. Television and high-powered publicity had been linked to skilled investigation methods. But in another sense the mainspring had been much simpler. What had finally convinced 285 M.P.s were not the television programmes and newspaper articles, but the sense of shock and outrage felt by ordinary people throughout the country.

On a crucial issue like that of the live food animals, the Society speaks not merely for itself. It speaks for the common humanity of the British people.

5 : The Modern Face of Cruelty

'In effect, we make the other animals into a slave class'
Brigid Brophy

'Perishable – Animals'

The way we treat animals now: consider the story of Sam, the spider monkey. When he was a few weeks old Sam was caught in a Brazilian rain-forest. Monkeys fetch high prices in the zoos of Western Europe – along with half a dozen others Sam was squashed into a crate and sent by air to London.

When the plane touched down, the crate was opened at the RSPCA's London Airport Hostel. Separated from their parents, too young, crammed into an ill-ventilated box, Sam's companions were dying. Sam himself was taken care of by the staff at the Hostel – but who wanted one small, displaced spider monkey?

In the end things turned out happily for Sam, for the Hostel staff found a good home for him. But for many animals there is no such happy ending. Victims of one of the world's most dynamically expanding trades, animals are being hurtled around the skies of the world daily. Many will go to zoos and pet shops, others to laboratories. Today there is hardly a species that does not travel by air. If you count birds and fish, the yearly total of animal air travellers now exceeds the humans.

Despite the soaring increase in the trade, it remains almost unregulated. Squashed in crates, sometimes without food or proper ventilation, it is hardly surprising that many never reach their destinations alive. Most of the crates have only a simple label stamped on them – 'Perishable – Animals', as if the contents were a load of cheese.

Perishable. The word might sum the story up. Meanwhile, what can the RSPCA do?

'Actually, I think these birds are going to be all right.' Neville Whittaker, manager of the Animal Hostel at London Airport, ran an expert eye over a cage of love-birds. There were perhaps a hundred of them, peach-faced, green and chattering, crowded in a cage as big as a large briefcase. Behind the wire bars on the sloping front there was clean water in two scruffy looking white dishes: the floor of the cage itself was covered with droppings. 'If it hadn't been for us', went on Mr. Whittaker, 'I don't think they'd have made it.'

At the London Airport Hostel, milk bottles must be jumbo size.

'If it hadn't been for you?'

'Somebody forgot to book their flight.' It seemed absurd that any-one should have to book a flight for birds. 'They've come from Angola, and they're supposed to be going on to Japan. Because somebody's made a slip-up about booking their on-going flight, they would have had to stay here three days.' As it was, Mr. Whittaker said, he had been able to twist somebody's arm to get them on an extra cargo flight. But if there had been no RSPCA Hostel at the Airport there would have been nobody to change their water and feed them, and most of the love-birds would probably have died.

Caring for a cargo of a hundred forgotten love-birds is an everyday example of the Hostel's work. Certainly it is far from an extreme one. Talking in his office with the windows shut to drown the howl of jets, Neville Whittaker told me some of the basic facts about the Airport Hostel. When it was opened in 1952 it was handling 800 animals a month; now the figure is 80,000, or just on a million a year. Complete with kennels, a paddling pool for seals and penguins, and houses large

Another heartbreak job for the girls at London Airport.
If an aircraft carrying day-old chicks is delayed, they will have to be destroyed.

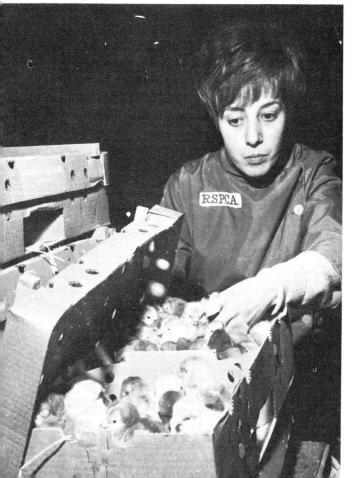

Due to bad packing, this tiger was dead even before
its air journey from London had begun.

enough to take a full-grown elephant, it represents a tiny complex of animal welfare in the world's most overcrowded airport. Some of the animals it deals with are coming to Britain direct, but many more will be in transit. When this happens, the Hostel staff will check the crates, change the food and water and if possible exercise the animals. For this it charges a handling fee to the airlines, which comes nowhere near to meeting the expenses. The £12,000 which the Hostel costs the Society every year is, in terms of welfare, some of its best-spent money.

I asked Mr. Whittaker just how bad the travelling conditions were? For example, how many of the million animals a year would die in transit?

'Nowadays it's less than half of 1 per cent, as compared with about 50 per cent when we started. The reason for this isn't because of more humane treatment, though. It's simply because the flights are quicker.'

Even so, it occurred to me, one-half of 1 per cent of a million is still 5,000 creatures. Also, the figure didn't take in terror, stress, misery, or the sheer unnaturalness of anything from a baby elephant to a goldfish being rushed around the world by man's most sophisticated transport. What, I asked, were the actual rules controlling the carrying of animals by air?

'Basically, the trouble is that there aren't any.' Mr. Whittaker, a small, energetic, bearded man, went over to one of the bookshelves which were crammed with well-thumbed titles like *Birds of Trinidad and Tobago*. He came up with a large folder and spread it on the desk.

'This is the International Air Transport Association Manual on the procedure for livestock in transit.' I glanced at the index in the front – every conceivable animal seemed to be listed, from avadavats to salamanders, crocodiles to crayfish. Below the index it said that this manual was intended as a guideline.

'That's just the trouble,' said Mr. Whittaker, 'it's got no teeth. The manual recommends what sort of crates the animals should go in, their feeding arrangements and so on, but it doesn't do more than recommend. Take those love-birds we were looking at just now – you saw those dirty little dishes? Well, let me show you how it should be.'

Mr. Whittaker leafed through the book till he got to 'love-birds': for these and various other categories of birds, the manual showed a drawing of a cage with sliding floors and removable water-dishes. 'If the shipper had followed the instructions here, we'd have been able to take out the bottom of the cage and clean the dishes properly. As it was, we had to siphon out the stale water through the netting, then pour new water in the filthy dishes. I'll show you something else, though.'

130

He went over to the bookcase and got out a large brown envelope of photos. One of them showed a flamingo, with a broken neck. 'That flamingo got its neck crushed by the lid of the crate. Yet, if you look it up in the manual what does it say?' He turned up 'flamingo' in the index and found the page. 'Carriage of flamingos and other long-legged birds. The height should be sufficient to permit the bird to stand with the neck in a natural position.'

We flicked through some of the other photographs on the file. One showed five dead monkeys, squashed in a box smaller than a tea-tray.

Flamingos dead on arrival at the airport – their necks had
been trapped over the partitions of the case.

'It hadn't even got any holes in the box', said Neville Whittaker. 'Those monkeys were virtually dead before they set off. There were a couple of apples on the floor of the box. The animals died before they got a chance to eat them.'

These were only some extreme examples. In Mr. Whittaker's time at the Hostel he has taken in a squirrel from Formosa that had been cocooned in chicken wire, then wrapped in a cigarette carton. Not all the worst cases come from abroad. One English zoo was sending two tigers in a box to Turkey: because they had so little ventilation one was dead on arrival at Heathrow and the other failed to respond to veterinary treatment and died. Nor are all the animals exotic ones: suppose a cargo of day-old chicks is travelling from America to the Middle East. If the aircraft is for some reason held up, the chicks will have to be destroyed, which means another heartbreak job for Mr. Whittaker's team of teenage girl helpers.

If the IATA regulations exist, I asked, why does nobody enforce them? Mr. Whittaker heard out the question with the air of a man who has fought a good many battles. 'Because it's a world where animals don't count. If an airline wants to run a cut-price trip to America, it's IATA that says it mustn't. But when it comes to the life of an animal, it doesn't seem to matter.'

'Isn't there anything you can do direct, through the airlines?'

'We can, and our relations with the airline cargo officials are very good. If there's something wrong, we put our view forward and they'll do their best to get it changed. The trouble is they can't answer for their counterparts in, say, Bangkok.'

'Bangkok being an example of somewhere where the animals are loaded?'

'Exactly. You get some local animal trader who's got a crate of monkeys for shipment to a zoo in Western Germany. He can cram them into the most appalling crate practically without food and water. Then he takes it along to the local cargo manager at the airport. The cargo manager *could* refuse to take it, and if he went according to the IATA book he ought to. But the chances are he won't, because he doesn't want to lose trade for his airline. If he won't take it, one of his competitors will.'

'What about the regulations when the animals get to London?'

'There aren't any regulations. The airlines know us, of course, and if an animal cargo comes in, the chances are they'll bring it over. But they don't have to.' Mr. Whittaker waved a hand in the direction of the long row of buildings along the airport skyline. 'There could be a lot of suffering animals in those freight sheds right now. If BEA get an animal

These monkeys travelled from Africa to London
in a case made only of wire and hessian.

The London Airport Hostel. A BEA stewardess
gets to know one of her passengers.

One of the Hostel's tragic cargoes. This whole consignment
of 3,000 finches from India were dead on arrival at the Airport.

in transit from another airline, their staff'll bring it over. Other airlines will keep a cargo for ten hours without doing anything about it. We'll often get a call from some tender-hearted loader who says do we know there are a lot of parrots sitting around, half suffocated, in a freight shed.'

'Do you often have rows with the airlines?'

Mr. Whittaker grinned and said he wouldn't exactly put it like that, but sometimes he was in a position to exert a little pressure. 'Supposing you get a lion cub that's inadequately boxed, and it's got to wait a couple of days before going on to Chicago. We'll insist on its being reboxed.'

'Supposing the airline says they don't want to go to the trouble and expense?'

'Then I'll tell them I'll have to call in the local RSPCA Inspector. And I'll gently remind them', said Mr. Whittaker with an air of modest caution, 'that if I do that it'll be very hard to keep it out of the press. After all, the last thing they want is a picture in the *Daily Mirror* of a baby lion cub, shown as the victim of some greedy airline. So they'll agree to its being boxed properly.'

Exotic animals are not the only victims. This dog had been sent in a case smaller than itself, and been accepted by the airline.

Not the least of the necessary attributes to those who work at the Airport Hostel is courage – recently Neville Whittaker had the unenviable task of administering a hypodermic to a tiger which had got loose in the cargo hold of an airliner. Another time he got an emergency call to say that a four-foot gaboon viper was loose in an aircraft's hold. 'It can be a fairly nasty moment when the door of the hold is closed behind you. You're in that great dark hold all by yourself with a snake, some crates, and a lot of mail bags.' Armed with an electric torch, protective clothing and a special grasper, it took Whittaker over an hour to find it.

The Hostel had to cope with a hazard of a different kind one day in 1972 when two dogs, separately crated, arrived from India on their way to the United States. As often happens, the staff decided the boxes were too small for humane transport, and asked the airline to replace them with larger ones for the next stage of their journey. The airline did so, and the two dogs were duly sent in the new crates to complete their journey to New York.

A fortnight later one of Whittaker's assistants asked him what she should do about destroying the original crates. The usual practice at the Hostel is to burn them, but in the case of the two dogs the crates had metal strips along the top; before the crates could be burned the strips would have to be removed. When the metal was torn off, it revealed that beneath each strip, there was a cavity, and within the cavity were some small packets. When the boxes were investigated by the Airport police, they found that each of the two had been carefully packed with £35,000-worth of cannabis.

The final irony of the London Airport story is that there is one class of animal which does travel properly – those destined to end on the experimenter's bench. In 1961, Mr. Whittaker toured both Africa and India to set up a code of packing for traders supplying the big pharmaceutical firms. 'If a laboratory orders a hundred monkeys, they want them to arrive in decent shape, and nowadays they do.'

Much the worst victims of bad packing are those whose eventual purpose is to entertain and delight the visitors to the world's zoos, most of whom would claim to be animal-lovers. When the first laws were framed against cruelty in England, at least those who broke them had the excuse of poverty and ignorance, but we have no such excuse.

The cruelties the Airport Hostel does its best to counter are born of a different attitude – the attitude of a society that sees animals as playthings.

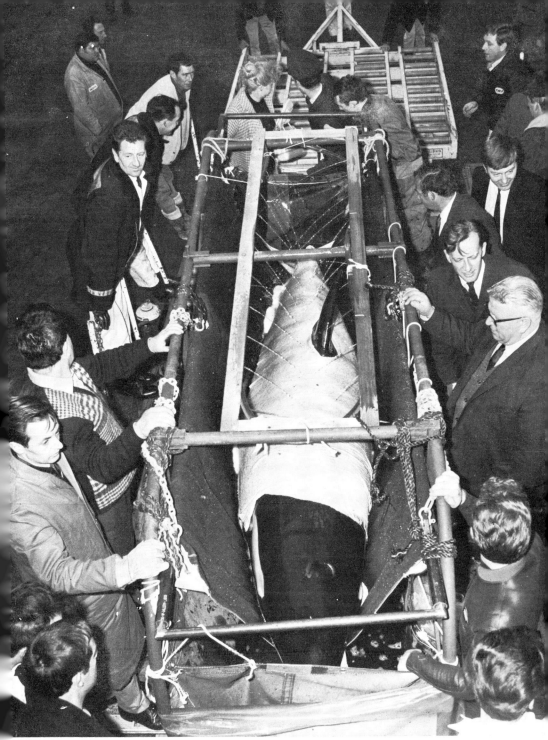

Stop-over for a killer whale. This one was in transit
to a zoo in the north of England.

The Jungle on the Doorstep

The scene is a leafy English lane. A line of cars moves slowly forward and then stops. The reason for their stopping is not the usual traffic-block at a beauty spot on a summer Sunday. It is a baby lion cub.

Moving out from the green verges it pads up to one car, leans engagingly against the door, then sniffs. From the safety of closed-up windows the occupants beam and glow with pleasure. When they get home they will not only have a car sticker to show that they have seen the lions – their car will actually have been licked by one. The jungle, you might say, is on their doorstep.

For thousands of families like this, the safari park is Britain's latest animal attraction. After all, surely safari parks must be more humane than any ordinary zoo, with its decrepit-looking lions patrolling narrow strips of concrete, and birds of prey shuttered in tiny cages? In the world of the safari park, the argument runs, we are seeing animals in the actual state they live in.

But are we? And just how good are the conditions in the safari parks that have become such a booming business?

*

'As safari parks go, I'd say this wasn't a bad one. Once you accept that they should exist at all.'

Bill Jordan stopped his car and gave a professional glance at a squad of wallabies that seemed to be in training for the long jump. The safari park was one of the largest ones in the country. In the distance you could see the snack-bars, the post-card stands, and lines of cars. In one of the near-by paddocks a couple of white rhino squared up in ritual confrontation, then retreated. It seemed an odd setting for some of the world's most disappearing species.

'You mean you'd argue that they shouldn't?'

Bill Jordan nodded, then said that there were really two arguments about it. 'There's a factual argument that asks if the animals are well cared for. Then there's the philosophical argument which asks if they should be here at all. If you take the factual argument first, those wallabies look pretty happy. They've got a decent-sized run and a well-built house. And those cages have got the right facilities for catching and handling an animal if it's ill.' Where a lot of safari parks fell short, he added, was that they had no means of catching an animal when they needed to.

Bill Jordan is one of the RSPCA's more recent appointments. A soft-spoken Ulsterman with a quiet manner which conceals a total resolution, his interest in wild animals began when he was vet to Chester Zoo. From there he went to Persia and then to South Africa, where he taught veterinary science at the University of Pretoria. At the end of eight years he and his family came back. Not a specially political animal, he says, he just couldn't be comfortable with the way the Africans were treated.

On his return Jordan saw that the RSPCA were advertising for an Assistant Chief Veterinary Officer to specialize in exotic animals. He applied and got the job. In a way, he said, it was a new departure for the Society, and an example of its broadening interest in world animal welfare. In the last year, as part of a joint campaign by the RSPCA and the Beauty Without Cruelty movement, he had been to Ethiopia to investigate the treatment of the civet cat, a secretion of which is used in making perfume. Next month he was going to Switzerland to do a bit of private detective work about what looked like the smuggling-in of tiger skins to Britain.

In the time he has been with the Society, Jordan has helped to set up a new and high-powered committee on wild animal welfare. Eventually, he hopes, it will do as much for wild animals as the SELFA campaign did for sheep and cattle. Another of his short-term objectives is to get an improvement in the conditions in which wild animals are forced to travel. 'If we get this committee properly working, it ought to be able to lean on the airlines till they stop the sort of things you heard about at London Airport.'

Meanwhile Jordan sees safari parks as being at the centre of what he calls wild animal exploitation: basically, his job, he says, must be a gradual attempt to raise standards. In the comparatively brief time he has been with the Society, he has toured more than twenty safari parks and zoos. 'More than half, especially the smaller ones, are sub-standard. I could take you to a place in the north where you'd see a lion in a cage where it can hardly move, and a lot of deer shut up in a little paddock where everything's been trampled down. That happens where you get somebody trying to make a living out of his animals, with not enough resources.'

In one of the largest and best known parks, Jordan came across a case where a group of lions had attacked another one and killed it, then eaten it. 'Animals don't fight in nature – the only living creature who attacks and kills his own kind is man. The only reason why lions would attack another lion is because something was wrong with their social grouping in the park.'

Far from living in their natural surroundings as most people like to suppose, animals like monkeys often shiver with cold in the English climate. When conditions of stress occur from overcrowding, the common symptom is that they bite each other's tails off. At one safari park, a hippo broke the ice of a frozen lake and drowned in it. Even so, no English park has yet had a loss like that of one in Vienna, where two giraffes had died of cold in a recent winter. The reaction of the Austrian animal welfare people, which Jordan agrees with, was that you might as well bring over Negroes from central Africa and make them run around in loincloths in a blizzard.

If the RSPCA want to make a complaint about conditions in a safari park, what are their actual powers? Basically, animals in British zoos and parks are protected by the same laws as any others, though cruelty can be more difficult to prove. Under the present law, neither zoos nor safari parks have to be regularly inspected, though a new law to be brought before the Commons may enforce this.

Meanwhile Jordan himself admits, not looking too distressed about it, that he has personally been warned off several safari parks. In other cases he has been along with a Travelling Superintendent, investigated conditions and made suggestions which the management has taken up. In one safari park, for instance, he found that around a hundred monkeys were being shut up at night in a cage not much bigger than a family garage. 'There wasn't enough shelf space for them all to sit, he says. 'The monkeys were sitting shivering in their own filth on the ground. We made a complaint, and it was acted on promptly. Now the number has been reduced by a quarter, and none of the animals is locked out at night.'

By now we had travelled perhaps three miles through the safari park, moving from one reserve to another where there were lions, cheetahs, tigers. Jordan looked at one of the tigers asleep. 'If you were really seeing him in his native state, they'd have to let you in the park at night. The tiger's a nocturnal animal.'

We moved on to the giraffes. Necks slanting downwards like a row of slipways, they were eating from the ground. 'When you see giraffes in Africa', said Jordan, 'they're always eating from tall trees.' One of his feelings about safari parks, he said, is that so much of the publicity is calculated to make the public think they are seeing animals in their natural state. Nowadays with cheap air fares, a lot of people could easily get to the East African reserves but were being siphoned off, deluded into thinking they'd seen the real thing in rural Britain.

'The true excitement of the African reserve isn't seeing the animals – it's the fact that you have to stalk them. You may go along seeing nothing for half an hour. Then somebody says excitedly, "look over there". And then your eyes get accustomed to the camouflage – against some brown thorn-bushes, or brown dead grass, you see a lion emerging.'

Ultimately, could this be the pattern of our zoos and parks in future? Jordan foresees the day when even in Britain they will be on a huge scale, with large geographical areas specializing in a single group of animals, not mixing them as at present. 'You get some African animals which adapt well, like wildebeeste and zebras. My idea is that you might get a few herds on a 700 acre estate in Scotland, then teach children how to stalk and observe them. You could keep a few herds of antelope at Whipsnade. The point is, if a zoo has a purpose at all, it's educational.'

Is Jordan's view of the safari park of the future a too austere one? In the end, he says, the argument is not merely about how much space you give an animal. 'When I was in Africa, I saw men degrading themselves by their treatment of black men. We in the West are doing the same with animals. In the end the argument's about the arrogance of man.'

The Indoor Farm

In the Society's early days, one thing was relatively simple. Cruelty was always done by someone else. It might be a cabdriver or costermonger whipping an exhausted horse through London streets or it might be a gang of thugs who organized a cock-fight. What would have seemed unthinkable to the early reformers was that they themselves bore responsibility for cruelty.

We all bear such responsibility today: what we must now turn to are some of the ways in which animals are exploited for our use. The first and most widespread example is the life, if it can be called life, of the animals on factory farms.

*

Pigs on a factory farm. *Opposite*, typical conditions for a veal calf.

Intensive farming is not in itself a new concept. Farmers have always sought to increase production by making the most effective and profitable use of land, animals and buildings. Even on a traditional farm the life of a calf which is slaughtered at eighteen months is not an enviable one. It will have been separated from its mother at an early age, horned, and castrated. On the other hand it can at least move around, swat flies and chew grass. It can live, as most of us feel it was meant to live, in the fields in a state of freedom.

Of course, a walk through a country lane will show you that many such animals still exist, munching away in English meadows. What we do not see is the other face of modern farming: the factory farms which have grown up during the last twenty or thirty years and in which animals pass their lives as virtual prisoners. Sometimes the factory farms are not in the open country at all, but on the edge of towns and even cities. Nor are they all run by farmers, but by industrial combines, quick to exploit the demand for more and cheaper food. Because their

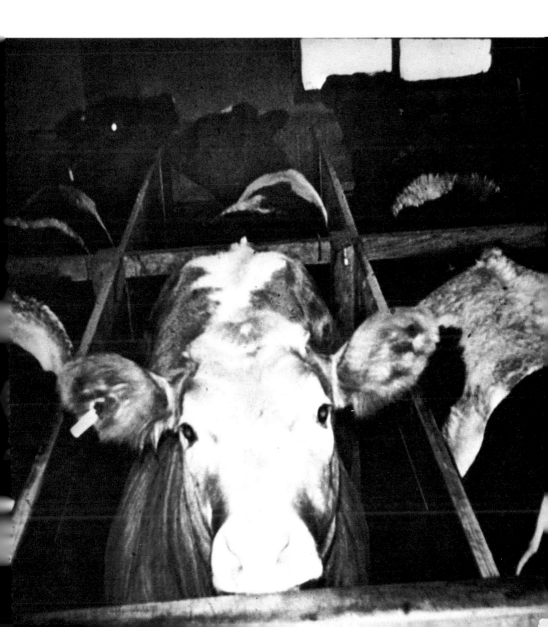

produce is cheap, thousands of us are able to eat, for instance, turkey and chicken, which even until about 1955 were comparative luxuries. Whether the quality or the taste is as good, does not concern us here. What does concern us is the price the animals are paying for our progress.

One of the first people to draw attention to the conditions on factory farms was a London housewife. Ruth Harrison knew nothing of the plight of the farm animals till one day a friend sent her a leaflet which depicted the sufferings of veal calves. As a vegetarian already, Ruth Harrison thought the leaflet hardly concerned her. Married to a successful architect and with two small children, her spare time was taken up with voluntary social work on a project for relieving loneliness in large towns.

A day or so afterwards she picked up the leaflet again. This time she realized it did concern her. That moment was the beginning of four years of research which took her to factory farms throughout the country. At the beginning she knew almost nothing of agriculture or veterinary science. By the time her research was complete, she had established herself as the major expert on factory farming in this country.

When her book *Animal Machines* was published by Vincent Stuart in 1964 it was hailed as a modern classic, serialized in *The Observer* and reviewed at length throughout the world. Many of the conditions she reported on were so extreme that one would have to go back to the records of eighteenth-century bull-baiting to match them. Consider this description of a poultry packing station given in her book:

Some packing stations have stunners to use before the birds have their throats cut, some do not. Some have stunners but do not use them. The one I visited was one of these latter. 'They do not bleed properly,' said the manager, 'it is much quicker this way, and kinder too.' I watched the birds having their throats cut and disappear flapping wildly, into the bleeding tunnel, to reappear a minute later still flapping wildly, to go into the scalding tank.'

Chickens are not the only victims. Ruth Harrison also described the condition of veal calves:

At the worst places I have visited the calves were kept in solid-sided crates no more than twenty-two inches wide by five feet deep. This is just big enough to house the calf standing, but barely enough to allow it to lie down . . . It was kept in the dark apart from two short

Factory farming of calves.

periods a day when a shutter is let down at the front of the crate for feeding. When we entered the building and the farmer switched on the light there was pandemonium from within the crates. He had to talk to a calf soothingly for many seconds before he dared to let down the shutter, and then there was no mistaking the misery on the face of this calf with its enormous staring eyes. The farmer himself seemed abashed and unhappy at the sight of it, but reassured himself with the remark that it produced top quality veal.

Such conditions exist in hundreds of factory farms today. The happy rural scenes on the advertisements for oven-fresh chickens do not mention the fact that the chicken will probably have been reared in a broiler-house where, packed in with thousands of others, it is allotted roughly the space of a sheet of quarto paper. (This example was quoted by Ruth Harrison to the British Association in 1968: the space had significantly diminished since she wrote her book in 1964, when the area was roughly the size of a piece of foolscap.) The chicken may also, to prevent it pecking other hens, have been de-beaked. This process, the unnaturalness of which is only matched by its cruelty, involves cutting with a hot knife through a section of tissue whose sensitivity is roughly comparable to that of the quick of a human nail.

In what are known as sweat-boxes, pigs live out their lives not only in darkness, but in a torpor induced by being kept permanently at a temperature of 80 °F. When you buy a veal and ham pie or a pot of meat paste, one of the ingredients is likely to be the flesh of unwanted male calves. Slaughtered at three or four days old, their brief lives are spent, says Ruth Harrison, in fear and hunger:

> The calf is separated from its mother at birth or a few days after. It is taken, often without a feed inside it, and bundled into the back of a truck, exposed to the cold and rigour of a market, to the cruelty of some drovers with their hobnailed boots and sticks. Neither the drovers, nor the boys who help them, appear to notice the distress of these young animals.

Why, ten years after the publication of Ruth Harrison's book, has so little been done to improve conditions? It is true that, on the eve of its publication the Ministry of Agriculture called a rather shamefaced press conference at which its chief scientific adviser said that in his view no case had been made out for 'making it an offence merely to deprive animals of light, freedom to exercise or pasture'. A different view was that of *The Guardian* in a leading article (9 March 1964), which warned that an increasing contempt for animal life could lead to a contempt for man himself. 'How big a step is it', the leader-writer asked, 'from the broiler-house to Auschwitz?'

Meanwhile the government, faced with the storm of public opinion raised by Mrs. Harrison's book, had set up a committee to investigate intensive farming methods, under the chairmanship of a distinguished F.R.S., Professor Rogers Brambell. When it reported in 1965, the committee's view was unequivocal: an animal, they said, should at least have sufficient freedom of movement to be able to turn round, get up, lie down and stretch its limbs. There should be a minimum size for pens and batteries. De-beaking and many other such processes should be banned.

But as so often before in the story of humane reform, official action was slow in coming. In 1967, following the Brambell recommendations, the Minister set up a standing committee to advise him on all aspects of farm animal welfare, including a careful assessment of both old and new techniques.

In 1968 a new Act was passed which redefined suffering on a wider basis, and also gave the Minister power to impose what are called Codes of Practice. Though these Codes are not mandatory as the Brambell Committee had suggested, they have some teeth: if a farmer applies for a Ministry grant, for instance, he will not get one unless conditions on his farm are approved. A further improvement came in 1970 with an Act which made it illegal to slaughter poultry without pre-stunning. On a European scale, the first steps towards an international policy came when the World Federation for the Protection of Animals submitted detailed recommendations to the Council of Europe.

What else can be done? Basically, the idea that reformers are up against is that so long as an animal is apparently thriving and getting fat, it cannot be said to suffer. Reformers, including the RSPCA, oppose this view. They say that the stress and anguish inflicted on the animal cannot be so measured. But how can the existence of stress in a calf or piglet be proved or disproved?

As a first step towards solving the problem, the RSPCA has now set up a high-powered study group, the Farm Livestock Advisory Committee, under the chairmanship of a distinguished anthropologist, Professor John Napier: among its other members are two farmers, a lawyer, two other zoologists and vets, and Ruth Harrison. A rotund, amiable academic from London University, Napier is about the last person you would take to be a member of the RSPCA (or for that matter of the Magic Circle, of which he was till recently vice-chairman). 'A lot of scientists', he says, 'would think the Society is an odd thing to belong to. I rather enjoy startling them.'

Originally, he told me, the idea of a study group on the subject had come from John Hobhouse, the Society's Chairman. 'Hobhouse wanted a committee which could view the problems of intensive farming objectively and put forward purely scientific arguments rather than emotional ones.' Meanwhile Napier admits to making one emotional judgment of his own since he saw the conditions in which veal calves are reared: he has given up eating white veal. 'And I used', he adds nostalgically, 'to love a wienerschnitzel.'

What can the Farm Livestock Advisory Committee actually do? 'What we want to discover', says Napier, 'is what sort of intensive farming practices cause stress in animals. In order to do this, we have to find a means of measuring stress. We believe this can be done by the assessment of abnormal behaviour – but what is abnormal behaviour and how do we recognize it? A large part of the Committee's work lies in answering those two questions.'

There can be several thousand birds in each shed of
a modern broiler-house.

In 1973 the RSPCA, in partnership with the Society for Veterinary Ethology, held the first purely scientific meeting in the RSPCA's history, an international conference on stress in farm animals. In addition to this, the Napier Committee has also established two annual research grants. The object of these is to initiate specific projects to compare the behaviour of animals under intensive conditions with those in ordinary farming. In 1973 the first two grants were made for studies in calves and pig-rearing. For the Society to take a scientific initiative of this kind, Napier believes, could be a major breakthrough.

Is it possible to hope for any immediate result? Though not everyone in the Society will agree, Napier's own view is that intensive farming is something we have got to live with. 'What we can hope for over the next few years is that the Committee will be able to stimulate a bit of action. For a start I'd like to see the worst of the existing methods abolished, where there's no doubt of their cruelty. After that no new techniques should be introduced until their effects have been tested and approved officially. This is a question not only of animals suffering, but of man's self-respect.'

One encouraging point for those engaged in the battle of the factory farms is that the farms are disliked by traditional farmers. An opinion poll after the Brambell Report showed that, where 87 per cent of people interviewed thought that animals should at least have room to turn in their pens, 85 per cent of farmers agreed. And as many as 72 per cent of farmers also opposed the basic factory principle by saying that animals should have natural daylight.

But in the end the issue is not only one for the farmers or the scientists: it concerns us all. 'Science has made it possible for us to treat animals as things', says Ruth Harrison. 'But because it is possible, does it mean we have the right to do so?'

Meanwhile there is one aspect of modern cruelty which is a much older story.

The Speciesists

Through most of the history of humane reform, animal experimentation or vivisection has been a fiery issue. Ever since Descartes had given the scientific world an assurance that animals had no souls, experiments on them had grown more widespread. Consider, for example, this famous passage from Samuel Pepys's Diary:

November 14th, 1666. – Dr. Croone told me, that at the Meeting at Gresham College to-night . . . there was a pretty experiment of the blood of one dog let out (till he died) into the body of another on one side, while all his own run out on the other side. The first died upon the place, and the other is very well, and likely to do well. This did

149

give occasion to many pretty wishes, as of the blood of a Quaker to be let into an Archbishop . . .

16th.   This noon I met with Mr. Hooke, and he tells me the dog which was filled with another dog's blood at the College the other day is very well, and like to be so as ever, and doubt not it's being found of great use to men, and so does Dr. Whistler, who dined with us at the Tavern.

All through the eighteenth and early nineteenth centuries such experiments had gone on. But what was becoming increasingly questioned was how often they were, as Pepys had put it, 'of great use to men'. 'The tortures inflicted in the dissection of living animals', wrote the Revd. Henry Crowe in 1824, 'equal, if they do not surpass, any of those practised in the Inquisition.'

Certainly the examples quoted by the anti-vivisectionists make lurid reading. In Paris, Professor Majendie, it was said, had nailed a spaniel by its ears and paws so that his pupils would get a better view when he came to saw its skull open and separate the eye-nerves. Another Frenchman, Brachet, wanted to discover the limits of a dog's attachment to its master. First he dug the dog's eyes out, then tortured it and still it licked his hand. Majendie used to stick needles into the backs of pigeons' heads, with the result that they walked backwards.

Though conditions in French and Italian laboratories were said to be the worst, those in Britain were not much better. One English researcher was said to have poisoned a cat with small doses of arsenic so slowly that it did not die for eighty days. Professor Fyfe of Edinburgh, according to one account, 'fastened a spaniel by all its feet, attached it still more surely by a stout thong which he put through the nostrils of the animal after he had made a hole through the nose with an iron instrument. He then cut open the chest and the belly to show his pupils the separate intestinal organs.'

What could the humane reformers do? At first the Society's opposition seems to have been merely token. In 1864 it offered prizes for the best essays on vivisection. In the face of the carnage in the laboratories the gesture may seem a little optimistic but was not without effect: among the prize-winners was a physician at St. Mary's Hospital, Mr. Markham, who said that anaesthetics should be used in all experiments and that many of those carried out by students were both cruel and needless.

By the 1870s, following the publication of the *Origin of Species*, experiments in biology were becoming far more frequent, but by now there was also widespread opposition. In 1874 there came what seems to have been the Society's first prosecution for needless vivisection. A French physiologist, attending a medical conference at Norwich, had injected absinthe into the veins of dogs. The RSPCA brought a case for cruelty: though it was dismissed, the Bench commended the Society's action and refused costs to the defendant.

Among those who were stirred by the Norwich incident was Frances Power Cobbe, an ardent Victorian reformer who had already done remarkable work among girl criminals in Bristol. Later Miss Cobbe was to become a suffragette and one of the Committee which helped push through that most crucial of women's rights, the Married Women's Property Act. Now, turning her attention to vivisection, she began organizing a vast petition, to be presented to the RSPCA. Working in somewhat unlikely partnership with the wife of a senior surgeon of St. Bartholomew's Hospital, she collected 1,000 signatures, ranging from those of the Archbishop of York and the Lord Chief Justice to Tennyson, Ruskin, and Carlyle. (Among the other opponents of vivisection, though she could hardly be expected to sign petitions, was an even more exalted figure. 'The Queen', wrote her Private Secretary to the Society on the vivisection issue in 1874, 'reads with horror of the sufferings of the brute creation.' Later, she was to refer to 'this horrible, disgraceful, and un-Christian vivisection'.)

In view of such pressure, the government could do little else but appoint a Royal Commission. Two years later, the first and only Vivisection Act ever to become law in England was passed. Basically, it specified that no animal could be experimented on without an anaesthetic, and that laboratories would be subject to Home Office inspection. On the other hand special licences could be obtained, often comparatively easily, by which an experimenter could get exemption from the Act's requirements.

Thus the reformers had gained the important point that experiments could only be carried out under law. What they had not gained was a law which was practically effective. 'The Act', wrote the Society's publication *Animal World* in 1877, 'is very unsatisfactory as a means for the discovery of offences, if not absolutely useless . . . It gives all but unlimited power over the lower animals to men whose humane feelings towards them are necessarily blunted by habit, or diverted by professional zeal . . .'

Today, almost a century later, that law still stands. Is there a modern case against vivisection?

Richard Ryder is senior clinical psychologist at a hospital in Oxford. The day I met him he had just come back from an anti-vivisection demonstration. Most of those taking part, he said, had been young people and other scientists.

How does a young and highly intelligent scientist come to be involved with such an unfashionable cause as anti-vivisection? Ryder himself prefers to talk about animal experimentation rather than vivisection. Literally vivisection means creatures being cut up, whereas many of today's experiments involve a subtler form of cruelty. Both as an undergraduate and a postgraduate, he told me, he had watched a great many experiments, and done some himself on rats. 'I had a bad conscience about it even in those days,' he said, 'but there was nothing we could do. In the 1960s there wasn't a squeak of opposition from the scientists.' Around 1968 Ryder's own opposition began to harden. Today he is one of a small but growing group of younger scientists who are dedicated to reducing the amount of experiments in our laboratories today.

Why should animal experiments have become, in the 1970s, once more a major issue? The first point to notice is the escalation of sheer numbers. When the original Act of 1876 was passed, something like 800 experiments a year were being done in British laboratories. By 1950 the number had risen to well over a million. Between 1950 and 1969 the annual total began to approach five million.

What appals Ryder is that many of these experiments are not even in the interests of medical science – animals are being used in their thousands, he says, in the testing of toiletries and cosmetics. 'Cosmetics testing is the prime example. You get a soap manufacturer who wants to find which sorts of soap are safest for humans. So chemists drop the soap in a concentrated form into the eyes of rabbits, without an anaesthetic. Can we honestly justify cruelty because someone wants to test a new deodorant?'

In the purely medical field Ryder also points out that many experiments are done by students. The most horrific thing he ever saw was at a university in California, where students had cut off a cat's tail and blinded it. 'Then they put it in a revolving wheel from which it couldn't emerge. They left the wheel turning for days and nights so it couldn't sleep. Every few hours they'd take it off the wheel, wrap it in a blanket so it couldn't scratch them, while one of them stuck a needle in its spine to draw off fluid from its brain. All this was in aid of some dim idea of finding out something about sleep-deprivation. They were

Animals for research.

pathetically low-grade students.'

Such an example may be extreme, but there are scores of other instances where students perform experiments simply to see effects already in the text-books. Because of the slackness of the law, Ryder says, many scientists have come virtually to the point where they treat animals as objects. 'One physiology student told me about a demonstration where a dog was bled to death simply to illustrate a well-known text-book phenomenon. The lecturer got hold of a friendly little dog, anaesthetized it and bled it to death so that half a dozen students could note the physical reaction to massive haemorrhage. All this can be seen on films, or in the text-books.'

To define the attitude implied by modern methods, Ryder has coined the word 'speciesism'. 'A racist is someone who thinks he can exploit other races, and a speciesist is someone who thinks he can exploit other species. In the eighteenth century many respectable merchants could run a slave trade using Negroes as their commodity. Their defence was that they were another race, and had no rights. Today many scientists mistreat animals and try to justify this by saying that animals are not the same species as ourselves, and so have no rights. But if Darwin was right, then the time has come for us to start treating animals as relatives, not as objects. If we were discovered by some more intelligent creatures in the universe, would they be justified in experimenting on us?'

Ryder reserves his strongest criticism for those experiments which are outside the field of medical research. Out of 5,000,000 in 1972, he claims, less than a third were obviously medical, with cancer research accounting for only $7\frac{1}{2}$ per cent of the total. Many of the rest were for such things as cosmetics, detergents, food dyes, and weapons research. In industrial research, thousands of animals are being forced to spend their lives inhaling dust, while in government warfare laboratories, monkeys are subjected to proton radiation. 'They get an idea of what it'd do to Russians', observes Ryder dryly, 'by irradiating rhesus monkeys.'

Even where animals are used in strictly medical research, Ryder claims they are not necessarily effective. He points to the fact that thalidomide was tested on animals in several countries without its

The rabbit is having experimental liquids dropped
in its eye to test a new shampoo.

terrible properties being discovered. 'On the other hand', he says, 'penicillin was never tested on animals at all. If it had been it would have shown a high toxic effect on guinea-pigs – which would have pretty certainly prevented its widespread use.'

Ironically, the huge rises in the numbers of experiments have come at a time when alternatives are becoming available. Tissue cultures, fertilized eggs, even sections of human intestines removed in operations, are being used in experiments which would previously have been done on animals.

How soon can we hope to see such methods put into wider use? Since 1972, Ryder has been a member of a special committee set up by the RSPCA on animal experimentation. Headed by Dr. Kit Pedler, himself a noted scientist and creator of the BBC *Doomwatch* series, the committee's first aim is to reduce the range of non-medical experiments, and second to increase the use of such alternatives as tissues. One of the reasons Pedler himself gave up a career in medical science was because he felt whole areas of experimentation were being done for what seemed to be scientifically irrelevant reasons.

Pedler does not go as far as Richard Ryder in condemning all experiments, but singles out those in such areas as cosmetics. 'The important thing for this committee to do', he says, 'is to find specific targets.' Another field where Pedler thinks unnecessary experiments are being made is in psychology. 'A lot of these', he says, 'are just bad science – with suffering being caused to reach a glaringly obvious conclusion. Somebody puts a baby ape in a cage with a foster mother, just to prove it isn't as happy as it would be with its real mother.'

In 1973 the committee also co-opted the widely respected Labour M.P., Douglas Houghton, who in the same year had presented a Bill which would require researchers, where possible to use such alternatives as tissues. Though the Bill failed its Third Reading, it attracted strong support both inside and outside the House of Commons. '5,500,000 animals annually', wrote *The Times* science correspondent at the time of Mr. Houghton's Bill, 'is accepted as too high by many research workers as well as by the anti-vivisection movement.'

The increasing disenchantment among scientists themselves was clearly shown by the number of applicants for grants from the Dowding Fund for Humane Research, which in 1973 offered awards amounting to £12,000 for researchers working without animals. The largest award, of £8,000, was made to Dr. Graham Richards, Fellow and Tutor in Physical Chemistry at Oxford University, for his research into a means of making tests on animals more selective. 'At the moment, perhaps 2,000 rats or monkeys might be used in testing the effects of

Insensitive to cold while drugged, this sheep is kept in an ice-bath.

the part one molecule plays in the whole effect of a drug', said Dr. Richards, quoted in *The Guardian*. 'By means of calculation in advance, one should be able to get it down so that only, say, 50 animal tests need to be made.'

Ultimately, it seems only a question of time before the availability of other methods will offer a way out of the moral problem. Probably only a few dedicated spirits would go the whole way with Richard Ryder and say that knowledge acquired by torturing animals is knowledge which man should not seek to gain. Meanwhile there is a rapidly growing awareness that neither the laws, the scientists, nor our own consciences are perfect.

Model Army

People helping animals: Celia Hammond combines being one of Britain's best known models with membership of the Society's Council and running what amounts to virtually a one-woman RSPCA from her cottage in Kent. Ever since she was a child she has loved animals and felt an instinctive need to help those in distress. 'Sometimes I wish I didn't get so concerned about them', she says. 'I'd enjoy my life a lot more if I didn't.' Enjoy it or not, few people have made such an impressive contribution to trying to solve the ever-increasing problem of too many cats: for the last ten years almost all her leisure time has been spent in neutering and re-homing unwanted cats and kittens, often helping their owners with money and transport. Ultimately she believes it is the only answer to the problem – what she would really like is for the RSPCA to insist on all bitches and cats leaving a branch home to be neutered.

Celia Hammond's toughness in the animal welfare cause might come as a surprise to people who only know her fragile features from the pages of *Vogue*. But in one way her unique position has helped her combat one of the more squalid trades in modern animal exploitation – the trapping and killing of wild animals for fur.

In the early days of her modelling career Celia Hammond often modelled fur coats, but never owned one herself. The point attracted a good deal of press publicity, and one newspaper story caught the eye of Lady Dowding, widow of the Battle of Britain commander, and founder of the Beauty Without Cruelty movement. Would Celia go, she asked, to see an actual seal-hunt in the Gulf of the St. Lawrence River? If so, Lady Dowding felt, it could create massive publicity and concern about the cruelty of killing seal pups to make fur coats.

For this ermine, death will be the only release –
though sometimes a trapped animal will bite a limb off to get free.

Although an ice-bound river where 50,000 baby seals were being clubbed to death was about the last place you would expect to find a *Vogue* model, Celia Hammond agreed to go. 'I didn't want to go one bit because I'm very squeamish. I felt I'd probably burst into tears or something. All the same I had to try.' In the spring of 1970 she and another Beauty Without Cruelty Council member, Jean Lefevre, set off to Canada and were taken by plane to the Magdalen Islands which were the centre of the seal-hunt. One local expert on seal-hunting told Celia that life on the Magdalen Islands was so boring that the hunt was the highlight of the year. 'He said if it wasn't for the relief of tension from the violence, they'd probably be murdering each other.'

As the plane got near the scene of the hunt, she remembers the beauty of the ice in the brilliant sun, then seeing that it was stained with blood.

In the course of that day Celia saw around fifty seals clubbed to death

Real People Wear Fake Furs. RSPCA supporters Virginia McKenna
and Bill Travers show that artificial furs can be just as stylish.

with long wooden clubs shaped like baseball bats. A large number, she thinks, were skinned alive. 'There were some that had been clubbed and skinned, and when I went over to them ten minutes later their hearts were still beating. A few were killed instantaneously, but many weren't. Sometimes when a seal was still moving the men would say it was reflex action, but it wasn't. I saw many baby seals making a conscious effort to escape from the hunters after being clubbed several times. That's not reflex action.'

From the point of view of the seal-hunters, the presence of the two girls clearly added zest to the scene. 'I think they hoped I was going to burst into tears but I managed to look calm. Looking back, I don't know how I did it. Normally if I see anyone being cruel to an animal I fly at them. I thought I'd probably make a fool of myself, but I knew it was important that I didn't.'

The publicity that followed the girls' visit was possibly one of the most decisive factors in influencing what has become an increasing public revulsion from the fur trade. In Canada they did six television interviews, gave a press conference on their return to London Airport, and were on the front page of the *Daily Mirror*. Celia Hammond believes that today the climate of public opinion is coming round still further.

A coyote with its leg caught.

'When I started refusing to model furs I felt very lonely. People simply didn't care. Now, very few girls will model sealskin. *Vogue* won't publish pictures of certain furs. There's a stigma attached to a real fur coat, and that's the way it should be.'

Celia Hammond adds one other point to the story. Because of the modern interest in conservation, she says, a lot of people get concerned about species which may be in danger of dying out, but forget about the more everyday animals. 'People worry about leopards and tigers, but don't give a thought to humbler animals killed for fur. Think of the life of a mink, spent in a cage till the day it dies. Or other wild animals caught in traps where the trapper doesn't come back for weeks or even months, by which time the animal has either died of starvation or been killed by predators.'

'This is the point where I part company with the conservationists. In the end we've got to be just as much against wearing a rabbit coat as one made from the skin of a tiger.'

6: A Chapter of Accidents

The north wind doth blow,
And we shall have snow,
And what will poor Robin do then?

Traditional

The Mountain World of Gerry Elmy

'I see Charlie's got himself a mate.'

'Charlie?'

Inspector Gerry Elmy slowed down his blue Ford Escort van and nodded. On the calm waters of Lake Tal-y-llyn two swans moved like galleons, half a dozen cygnets following behind them. The three peaks of Cadr Idris were etched sharply against a Wedgwood sky.

'Charlie's the cob swan. That means the male. We had quite a bit of trouble over Charlie.' Gerry Elmy stopped the van and switched off the engine. We got out, strolled down to the end of the lake and waited. He knelt down and clicked his fingers, but the fleet of swans merely described an extra semi-circle to inspect us, then wheeled back to the middle of the lake.

'They're wonderfully loyal birds.' Gerry Elmy watched them. 'That was really the cause of Charlie's trouble.'

We sat down by the lake and he outlined the story. Charlie, it seemed, had always been a great favourite in the valley. They had even got his picture in the bar of the Tal-y-llyn Hotel. In the evenings he would often stroll into the hotel kitchen there, collect anything that was going in the way of bits of food, then stroll out again.

But one day disaster had struck at Charlie's serene life in the valley. His mate, the pen swan, was sitting on her eggs when a summer visitor had come down with a Labrador, and the dog had started sniffing round the nest. The pen swan attacked the Labrador, and the dog's owner had gone for her with a stick. The incident had been seen by the local bus-driver, driving through the winding lanes beside the lake.

Inspector Elmy with Charlie the Swan.

On his return journey the bus-driver saw a dead swan by the nest. The inference was clear. The summer visitor, probably frightened for himself, had left the pen swan dead. The bus-driver went into the hotel and telephoned Gerry Elmy. The Inspector knew that swans were so loyal that, unlike most other wild creatures, they always mate for life. Even so he had not been prepared for what he found when he got to the lake side. Charlie was sitting on the nest himself, trying to hatch the eggs out.

For thirty-five days after that Gerry Elmy made the forty-mile round trip from Barmouth to the lake side, taking with him a mixture of corn and bread which he had soaked in water. 'The fear was', he said, 'that Charlie might starve to death as the weeds surrounding the nest got eaten up. Charlie would stroll away from the nest a bit when he got cheesed off with sitting, but he wouldn't go too far. I think he'd have died sooner than leave that nest.'

It can rain harder in the Merioneth valleys than in most places in Britain. Over the next month Gerry found himself going up to Tal-y-llyn in more and more atrocious weather. 'I didn't mind that for myself but the trouble was the eggs weren't going to hatch. As the weather became worse, they got more damp and cold every time Charlie sat on them. One day I decided that it was going to be no good. If we were ever going to get Charlie back to normal, we were going to have to take those eggs away.'

He had gone up with the handyman from the hotel, and while the handyman kept Charlie at bay, he had taken the eggs from the nest. 'It may sound cruel, but I think if I hadn't done that, Charlie would have sat there for ever.'

We looked across the quiet waters of the lake. Charlie was certainly back to normal now, cruising magisterially round with his new mate, the little flotilla of cygnets behind them.

'Did he find his new mate in the valley?'

'More likely from Portmadoc. There's lots of swans there in the

Sparky the Seal. He was back to sea shortly after this photograph was taken.

winter. He'll have flown over the mountains to get her, then come back with her.'

'How long would that take him?' I remembered the road to Portmadoc, forty miles away, twisting and turning round the edges of the Rhinog range of mountains.

'Maybe an hour or so. It's nothing for a swan.' He glanced up to the soaring flanks of Cadr Idris, its clefts alternately lit and shaded by the morning sun. 'A swan'll fly higher than an aeroplane sometimes. I've seen Charlie myself, high over the estuary, heading for the top of Cadr Idris.'

By now the swans were far over the lake, and it occurred to me there was something rather splendid in the thought of the lone swan's flight over the high mountains, his loyal task performed. Now he was back on the quiet waters of Lake Tal-y-llyn. It seemed the right setting for a happy ending.

As we drove on through the valley Gerry Elmy told me more about his world of birds and animals among the mountains. Based at Barmouth in Merionethshire, his patch covers more than two-thirds of the Snowdon National Park – nearly a thousand square miles of some of the roughest mountain country in Britain, where a missed footing can often lead to a sheep or a dog lying for days on some precipitous ledge.

What had brought Gerry Elmy to the RSPCA? Before he joined, he had been selling washing machines in his native Sunderland, then decided that the world of buying and selling was not for him. He had applied to become an Inspector, and been posted to Barmouth. Now he likes it so much he is not anxious for promotion. 'I must', he says with a grin, 'be the only Welsh-speaking Geordie in the Service.'

Every morning he sets off in the van from his house overlooking Cardigan Bay, and drives anything up to a hundred miles. It may be to pick up a couple of stray dogs, or to check the condition of the Shire horses that pull down the logs from the forestry plantations in the National Park.

Were there, I asked, special problems involved in working in a holiday resort like Barmouth? Gerry Elmy said the summer was always his busiest time. 'You get people bringing their cats and dogs in their caravans, and the animals run off and get lost. I had one chap the other day who'd lost his cat. He's been down from Liverpool every weekend for the last three weeks looking for it.'

Another thing he has to watch out for are the donkeys and ponies that give rides on the beach. Every day in August, he goes down to the beach to see they are not being overworked.

At the other end of the scale are the complaints of over-anxious holiday makers: 'You get a lot of people who come along and say that some farmer is overworking his dog, but most of the complaints are unfounded. It is very rare to find a Welsh hill farmer who will ill-treat his dogs, if only because they're his living.'

But the part of his work Gerry most enjoys is rescues. In his van he carries, not only the usual equipment of an Inspector, but a formidable assortment of nylon ropes, crash helmet, and karabiners, which are metal spring clips, and pitons. He has taken a course for his Mountain Leadership certificate and when I saw him he had just spent a week of his annual holiday at the Mountain Training Centre at Tywyn.

Not all his rescues have actually been on mountains – one of the most dramatic was when he descended sixty feet underground to rescue a seal. Later christened Sparky, it had got itself trapped in the water-cooling plant of the nuclear power station at Anglesey, and was swimming around in what was virtually a series of underwater caverns. To get him, Inspector Elmy and his helpers risked being sucked in by a rush of water moving at the rate of fifteen million gallons an hour: all the same, he managed to get the seal out. None the worse for his experiences, Sparky's picture appeared next day in all the local papers.

Meanwhile Gerry Elmy's most spectacular rescue came in 1973. Because of its scale and the hazards involved, the story is worth telling in a little detail. Also it demonstrates something we saw in the story of the Scarborough rescue. When an animal is in danger, it will be the RSPCA Inspector who initiates the rescue, and usually he will be the one who takes the largest share of danger.

But in a wider sense, major rescues are a team effort, for it is not the least of the Society's achievements to have educated public opinion. Today an animal in danger is a cause for everyone's concern.

*

One Saturday morning in April 1973 a sheep farmer named John Edwards set off looking for a fox on the hills adjoining his farm in the Cwm-pryssor valley. With him went his ten-year-old son Gareth and the family fox terrier, Bonzo. There are relatively few hunts in Wales. When a farmer suspects the presence of a fox, he will usually go out with his terrier and a gun. The idea is that the terrier sniffs out the fox, puts it up, and the farmer shoots it.

On this occasion Mr. Edwards had not seen the fox, but was pretty certain of its presence. A few days before, he had found a dead lamb stretched out on the grass. Mr. Edwards had decided there must be an old vixen somewhere about. So, on this particular Saturday morning, he, Gareth, and Bonzo had set out from the farm, with Bonzo jumping and barking with excitement as he always did at the sight of Mr. Edwards's gun. They had climbed almost to the summit of the two-thousand-foot mountain of Moel Slates, which lies behind the immediate hills forming the Cwm-pryssor valley.

After they had been walking for a couple of hours, Bonzo put up a fox, then chased it into what appeared to be a series of caves or tunnels in the mountain. From outside they heard what Mr. Edwards called 'a terrible commotion' of barking and fighting, but Bonzo did not come out.

There seemed nothing Mr. Edwards could do. He and Gareth waited for almost an hour, then reluctantly went home. Through the Sunday there was no sign of Bonzo returning. On the Monday morning, at one o'clock, he and his cousin who farms near by in the valley, went up with five dogs to the mountain. They sent the dogs into the burrow on Moel Slates. All five dogs reappeared, but Bonzo did not. Then, just as Mr. Edwards and his cousin were about to leave, they heard a sound of barking. Evidently Bonzo was alive, but had somehow got himself stuck in the tunnels.

The following day Mr. Edwards went back to Moel Slates yet again, this time with a gamekeeper from a neighbouring estate and ten dogs. As before, the other dogs went down, and reappeared, but Bonzo didn't. That evening Mr. Edwards decided to contact the RSPCA: by now he was doing almost nothing on his farm except to look for Bonzo.

'I'd taken the little dog up there. It was his job, of course, but it was me that took him. I couldn't get it out of my mind that it was my job to get him out.' He did not know the RSPCA Inspector personally, but he had often read in the local papers about his rescues of sheep from the mountains. Mr. Edwards's mother and stepfather, who farm farther down the valley, also knew Gerry Elmy from Dolgellau market.

Once the RSPCA had been contacted a comprehensive range of rescue services swung into action. Because Inspector Elmy is known in the valleys as a skilled mountaineer who will go out in any conditions in any emergency, local climbing clubs will always do the same for him. But on this occasion not only climbers but pot-holers were needed.

Part of the team which failed to rescue Bonzo.

Gerry Elmy assembled his team, and on the Wednesday there began one of the most intensive animal rescue efforts ever mounted. 'What we had to do', he says, 'was literally to burrow ourselves inside the mountain to try to get into the cave where we guessed Bonzo must be stuck.'

Wearing helmets fitted with battery-powered lights, the ten-man team began to crawl through a passageway two feet wide by eighteen inches. They formed a human chain to shift the rock, and by the end of the first day had shifted almost a ton of it. Most of the time the rescuers had to lie on their stomachs and ease themselves forward through a mixture of mud, and what pot-holers call black damp.

'The worst part', says Gerry Elmy, 'was looking at the roof, seeing those horrible rocks with no visible means of support. Every rock we'd dug out was making it more unsafe. I just used to look at it and think "God, how much longer can it stay there?"'

Meanwhile what kept the rescuers going was that there were still sounds of life from Bonzo. Mr. Edwards had heard barking from outside, up to the fifth day. As late as the eighth day of the search, Gerry Elmy and one of the pot-holers had heard a faint whimpering from somewhere through the rock. The team was now augmented by members of the Outward Bound Sea School from Towyn. Rescuers worked for two-hour stretches, except for some of the pot-holers who worked four hours without a break. 'We had a hell of a job to get them to come out to the surface at all', says Gerry. 'By this time the whole valley only had one object – to bring out Bonzo.'

By the Friday morning the team had burrowed forty-five feet inside the mountain and reached the cave. By now, the pot-holers warned them, the subterranean channels had been so loosened that there was serious danger of the cave-roof falling in. That evening the rescuers held a conference at Mr. Edwards's farm. Now they had pinpointed the position of the cave, they decided, what they needed was a mechanical digger to approach the cave from above.

From Mr. Edwards's farm, the police sergeant from Blaenau Ffestiniog spent most of the next morning on the telephone. Finally, he got hold of the Forestry Commission, who had a JCB mechanical digger available, and were willing to lend it free. Once again, it was a question of the RSPCA man being well known in the valleys – in the past Gerry Elmy had often helped the Forestry Commission by keeping an eye open for forest fires while doing his rounds in his van.

Next morning the Forestry Commission's JCB arrived in the Cwm-pryssor valley from Beddgelert. Then began the difficult ascent of three miles of rough mountain country almost to the summit of Moel Slates. At half-past two in the afternoon the driver began digging. By half-past seven he had dug twenty feet down, a hole twelve feet by fifteen feet. Fanning out from the hole, the rescuers could now see a series of passageways. They began searching them, burrowing into them with picks and shovels, and shining torches. There was still no sign of Bonzo.

By now the JCB driver had worked five hours without a break. At 7.30, it had been decided, further attempts should be postponed until the morning. Then, suddenly, the JCB's grab struck a new channel. The rescuers, who had been on the point of going home, began to clear it. Fred Owen, a gamekeeper from down the valley, put his arm inside. The search was over, and what they had found was heartbreaking after all their effort.

Jammed in the narrow passage of rock, both animals had perished in the wild justice of the mountains. Almost locked against the vixen's body was that of Bonzo. Fighting to the last, the little dog had cornered the vixen, killed her, then found his exit blocked by his victim's body. Probably he had suffocated or starved to death the day after Gerry Elmy had heard whimpering from the tunnel.

A few weeks later I drove up the Cwm-pryssor valley to John Edwards's farm with Gerry Elmy. Mr. and Mrs. Edwards greeted us, gave us Eccles cakes and coffee while Gareth played with the new puppy, a six-week-old Jack Russell.

I asked Mr. Edwards how he had felt about the rescue attempt and he said that the outcome seemed hard after so much effort. At the same time there was the knowledge they had done everything they could. What he could not have done, he said, was leave Bonzo to his fate, not knowing what had happened. 'I'd go far if there's something suffering. Just like when we get sheep under snow in winter, we always go to them. We are on this earth to help things.'

Presently we strolled round the farm, looking at the sheep gathered under the looming brow of Moel Slates, across the valley. Mr. Edwards and Gerry Elmy talked again over the rescue and the friends they had made on it. Then Mr. Edwards said he thought of putting a little plaque on the mountain to commemorate the rescue.

'I thought I'd put something like "Bonzo. Brave little dog". Then something about the rescue attempt made by the RSPCA, something like that?'

'That'd be nice. You'd have to mention the Forestry', said Gerry Elmy. 'And the North Wales Caving Club. And the police of course, and Ned and Fred from down the valley.'

'And then there'd be the Outward Bound School. And the Snowdonia Warden.' It seemed an impressive list for one small fox terrier. 'Be nice for people to look at, when they feel like a bit of a walk up the mountain. Get a bit of fresh air, like.'

'They'll get that all right.' Gerry Elmy looked with feeling at the summit of Moel Slates. 'All the same, I'd do it again.'

In the Inspector's world, the final attribute is courage.

Hell and High Water

Anyone who has ever searched for a lost animal will know the feelings of the people in the Cwm-pryssor valley. But what about those cases where the lives of not one, but hundreds of animals are threatened?

When the North Devon flood disaster of 1952 engulfed the holiday resort of Lynmouth, thirty people died. Homes and hotels were wrecked as heavy boulders, brought down by the swollen river Lyn, crashed down on the holiday town. One aspect that might have been forgotten, had it not been for the RSPCA, was that in their evacuated homes, many families had had to leave their pets behind them.

What, in the context of the almost total destruction of a town, could the RSPCA do? When Inspector John Ambrose arrived at Lynmouth on the morning of the flood, the scene that confronted him was a grim one. 'There were cottages swept away and water all over the streets. At one stage we were walking over boulders weighing a ton, with buried cars beneath them.'

Ambrose set off down the hill in waders with two or three cat-baskets and started rescuing what animals he could find. By the end of the morning, helped by Inspector Pickett from Exeter, he had made a dozen trips up and down the hill – the gradient is one in three – and had got twenty-nine cats safely in his van.

Soon the police were keeping him informed with lists of missing or abandoned animals. 'When a family was evacuated, they'd tell the police what pets they'd left behind. Then it was just a question of my going into one flooded house after another and bringing out some pathetic creature.' One dog was so terrified of water after the flood that it was nearly six months before he could even walk beside a river. Even so, Ambrose remembers with pleasure that not a single animal was put down.

Other areas have their special local hazards. On Dartmoor the enemy is snow. In the exceptionally severe winter of 1962, helicopter pilots from the RAF Station at Culrose broke their Christmas leave to help a team of twenty RSPCA Inspectors to ferry loads of hay to stranded sheep and horses. Even in an ordinary winter, there are many days when the Plymouth Inspector will need to be on the Moor from dawn to dusk. Superintendent Henry Forward, now of the Head-quarters staff, spent ten years there. This was his account of a working day on Dartmoor:

It's when the weather begins to settle that we'd go out looking for the buried sheep. When the snow's actually falling, there's nothing you can do. However well you know the Moor, you'd get lost in five minutes. Most times I'd go up with another Inspector and a team of Dartmoor commoners. We'd take anoraks and waders, and fifty yards of lifeline. The point of the lifeline is that you can rope

RSPCA men and farm workers rescue sheep from floods on

yourselves together if there's another blizzard. Once you're up there, you work all the hours of daylight looking for the sheep. You might get half a dozen blackfaced sheep stuck in a gert, which is what they call a dyke. What happens is that they'll go for shelter to the leeward. Only the trouble is, that's the side that the snow blows and covers everything . . .

Sometimes you get a blowhole – where their breath has blown a little tunnel. Once you see the blowhole you know there are live sheep there, and you all start digging. If you can picture a drift it comes over the top and down. So you have to dig down sideways, and if you're lucky you'll find them perhaps twelve feet down and you can lift them out without a block and tackle.

If you're not lucky, you'll find they've sheltered in a hole or a pit of some sort. If you look at the Moor when it's been snowing everything looks white and smooth, but there's a whole heap of tin mines and old quarry shafts where you can fall a hundred feet . . . It's a job for specialists, all right. All the same, I miss it.

Exercise Beauty Box

Ralph Gardner of Truro could almost be described as the archetypal RSPCA Inspector. Sturdy, tanned, with a Jack Warner-ish look of dependability, he is also much liked by the Cornish. (They still sometimes talk about foreigners in his presence, he says, forgetting that, being a Taunton man, he is one.) Such characteristics stood Ralph Gardner in good stead when, in March 1967, he faced the worst disaster to natural life that has ever happened on an English coast: the sinking of the *Torrey Canyon*.

Younger readers may like to be reminded of the facts. The *Torrey Canyon* was an oil tanker, bound from the Middle East for Milford Haven in Wales. On the night of 17 March she struck a reef between Land's End and the Scillies, known as the Seven Stones. In her holds were 120,000 tons of oil. The fear – and very soon the reality – was that the oil would flood out from the stricken ship and contaminate beaches along the Bristol and the English Channels.

When Ralph Gardner heard the news of the *Torrey Canyon* he was, like everyone else in Cornwall, horrified. Oil slicks along the coast would mean smells, filth, probably a loss of income in the forthcoming holiday season. What did not immediately occur to him was that he

Snow on Dartmoor.

might be professionally concerned. Like all coastal Inspectors, Gardner had from time to time had to deal with the occasional oiled seabird, but no disaster on a major scale had ever happened.

Meanwhile, one man had thought of the grim possibilities that the *Torrey Canyon* oil could have for seabirds. Soon after the first news of the tanker's grounding, Superintendent Kerr, based on RSPCA Headquarters in London, had rung Inspector Gardner. Just in case of large numbers of birds being affected, he said, he was sending a standby team to Cornwall. At Mousehole, just along the coast from Penzance, the RSPCA had a small sanctuary, mostly used for treating injured gulls. Inspector Gardner set it up as best he could as an emergency station and waited.

By now, despite continual spraying with detergent by the Navy, huge patches of oil were drifting eastwards up the English Channel. On the Easter Sunday morning, the 26th, the first oil began to come ashore at Marazion, famous for its local landmark of St. Michael's Mount.

Gardner still recalls his first sight of Marazion beach with horror: all along it the sea was bringing in thick sticky oil. Floundering in it, sometimes even stuck by it to the stones, were hundreds of birds – guillemots, razorbills, and puffins. Almost adding to the confusion

175

were the people trying to help. At one stage, Gardner recalls, there were so many that the police and RSPCA men had to turn them back. 'People were picking up as many birds as they could, packing them in their cars, and taking them off to Mousehole. What was fantastic was the way that everyone just felt they had to help. I remember one girl who'd come down to the beach to swim. By the end of the day she was plastered and covered with oil. She looked like some bedraggled gipsy.'

So far the oil was only coming ashore on the south coast – but what if one of the slicks drifted up the north coast, along the Bristol Channel? Here there would be a risk of far greater numbers of damaged birds, for out to the west of the Bristol Channel there were huge colonies of razorbills and guillemots.

Working non-stop at Marazion, Gardner did not know that what he feared had already begun to happen. During the Sunday afternoon people on the cliffs at Perranporth, on the north coast, had seen a dark, brownish mass discolouring the sea. As the wind blew it landwards, some people in the town were literally sick with the smell.

Oil-polluted seabirds. Thanks to modern research,
many will be completely cleaned and returned to freedom.

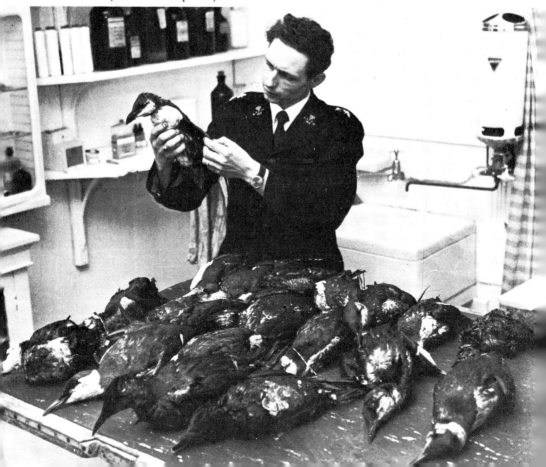

That night four or five oiled guillemots were washed up on Perranporth beach. It was only the prelude to what was to come. Among the first people on the beach next morning was Leslie Hicks, the proprietor of the Beauty Box, a hairdresser's shop on the seafront. Looking along the three-mile beach, Mr. Hicks saw a floundering mass of seabirds, some so drenched in oil that he could not tell their species. By now Inspector Gardner had also arrived in Perranporth, and within hours an emergency cleaning station had been set up on the seafront.

'The first thing', explains Mr. Hicks, 'was to get rid of any oil the bird had swallowed. You had to open the bird's beak and examine its throat to see if it was stained with oil. If so, we'd give it three drops of castor oil from a dropper. Then we'd thoroughly clean the bird in detergent, rinse the suds off, and wrap it in a cloth.'

At the cleaning station on the front there now began a two-way traffic. One team of volunteers brought heavy cans full of hot water. Another team of car volunteers took cleaned birds to a large double garage where they were dried in front of heaters. 'It seemed a strange thing for birds that live in the wild,' says Mr. Hicks, 'but what affected them most was the cold. They just sat huddled together for warmth.'

By the Monday night 240 birds had been cleaned, but the volunteer team had come to one conclusion. Bringing the heavy cans of water several hundred yards was too laborious a process. To add to the problems, well-meaning sightseers were getting in the way. But what was essentially needed was somewhere indoors with running water.

It was at this point that Hicks thought of his own shop: the Beauty Box was on the front, close to the beach, and well equipped with basins. He and his wife talked it over, and put the idea up to the rest of the volunteers. They would set aside one room for hairdressing, and use the other three for cleaning birds.

For the next few days what was normally a sophisticated hairdresser's shop became a hospital for oiled seabirds, with all the filth and smell that that entailed.

Three of Mrs. Hicks's girl assistants worked at cleaning. When a bird needed to be put out of its misery, Dr. Speed, the local G.P., injected it with a hypodermic. To feed those that seemed to be recovering, carloads of sprats were brought from the fishing port of Newlyn. Inspector Gardner brought in detergent in ten-gallon cans.

For the volunteers themselves, the process of cleaning was not merely exhausting and filthy but often painful. 'Opening a razorbill's beak isn't a job you can do with gloves', recalls Leslie Hicks. 'Most people's hands were sore with being pecked.' One evening he counted the pecks on his own hands and arms. He had 84 peck marks below the elbow.

For the RSPCA Inspector, nothing is too much trouble. If a fire brigade ladder is the only way to get a cat down a tree, then the Fire Brigade is asked to help.

Among the most eager helpers were children, who brought birds in by the dozen. Ralph Gardner remembers seeing one nine-year-old sitting on one of the crates used to carry the seabirds. 'He was so exhausted he'd fallen asleep. For me, the sight of that one child summed up the story.'

Exercise Beauty Box continued for three weeks – then, around 10 April, the numbers of birds coming in oiled began to dwindle. On 17 April, the Beauty Box closed as a cleaning centre, and Mr. and Mrs. Hicks began the long, expensive and arduous process of turning it back into a hairdresser's shop. In three weeks more than 1,000 birds had been treated in Perranporth alone. Most, like those from other Cornish beaches, were eventually taken to Mousehole or the RSPCA's Animal Centre at Little Creech, near Taunton. Here the great majority stayed for several months, undergoing a long process of rehabilitation.

Once the birds were cleaned, you may be thinking, why could they not be released at once? Why was it necessary for them to be kept captive for long periods of convalescence? The point is that a seabird produces natural oil from its own body. It is this oil which keeps it warm, and enables it to float and swim in the wild waters of the Atlantic.

Very little was known at the time of the *Torrey Canyon* about how this process worked. Ornithologists had assumed that the cleaned birds would soon produce their natural oil, but in the event they did not do so. Sadly, the final phase of the *Torrey Canyon* story is that the great majority even of the cleaned birds died. Out of 8,000 birds rescued from Cornish beaches after the disaster, Inspector Gardner reckons, not more than 500 survived to be released.

But, happily, it is not the end of the story. After the *Torrey Canyon* disaster a special unit was set up at Newcastle University to investigate the rehabilitation of oiled seabirds. Headed by Professor R. B. Clark of the University's Zoological department, the unit was formed with help from the RSPCA and the Royal Society for the Protection of Birds, among other bodies. Research began at once on seabirds not only from the *Torrey Canyon*, but those oiled in all pollution incidents throughout the country.

By June 1972 Professor Clark and his team were able to announce a substantial breakthrough. What had not been known at the time of the *Torrey Canyon* was that the cleaning method used was leaving a thin film of detergent on the birds' feathers. This, the researches showed, had reacted on the birds' own natural oil – as fast as it made the oil, the detergent destroyed it. Using new cleaning methods, Professor Clark found that it was possible to remove the last trace of detergent. By

1972, he was able to report, birds were being released to sea within a few weeks of cleaning.

Thanks to the lessons learned from the *Torrey Canyon*, it seems certain that in any future disaster far more birds will survive. But meanwhile the watch on the Cornish beaches goes on. An incident like the *Torrey Canyon* may catch the headlines and the national conscience. What most of us forget, or are not aware of, is that every winter thousands of birds round our coasts are dying cruel and unnecessary deaths.

Mostly the pollution is caused by tankers which, having discharged their cargo at a British port, clean out their bunkers at sea. As far back as 1964 international agreement was reached by the world's oil companies that this practice should be discontinued. Today most major oil companies insist that their ships' bunkers must only be cleaned in port: but others, in order to cut costs, continue the old practice.

'You get a tanker coming back from Milford Haven', says Inspector Gardner. 'Passing west of the Scillies, she'll swill out her bunkers. In the winter months, this is the area where the birds will be coming ashore for the breeding season. A bird sees a patch of discoloration on the water, and the ironic part is that it takes it for a shoal of fish. It dives straight into the middle.'

Because they have never forgotten what the seabirds suffered at the time of the *Torrey Canyon*, the people of Perranporth today keep constant watch. In their small garden on a winding lane above the cliffs, the local postman, Rex Harper, and his wife Julie have a small sanctuary where damaged seabirds can be cared for. From January to March eighteen-year-old David Robins makes a night patrol of the three-mile beach – for the last four years there has been scarcely a winter night when he has not come home from school, done his prep, and then gone down to the beach.

'Usually', he told me, 'I go down when the tide's receding, because there are likely to be some guillemots left stranded. That can mean going down at midnight. On a bleak winter night, it can be fairly spooky.'

If he finds a damaged bird, David will leave it in his father's garage overnight: in the morning his mother will ring Inspector Gardner, who will then collect it. Now in his last year at the local comprehensive school, David had first thought of becoming a vet. Now, though he has never thought of himself as being political, he told me he would like to work for some cause which could help to stop such forms of casual cruelty. 'If these tankers didn't discharge their oil simply to save harbour dues, none of this pollution would need to happen. The worst thing's knowing that it still continues.'

7 : Birds, Beasts, and Humans

Each outcry of the hunted Hare
A fibre from the Brain does tear.
A Skylark wounded in the wing,
A Cherubim does cease to sing.
William Blake

A Pocket Full of Redpolls

'Can I have a look at your birds?'

'What do you want to look at 'em for? They're very nice birds.'

'I know they're nice birds. That's why I want to have a look at 'em.'

Inspector Kenny, I noticed, had lost his beard. 'You need to look a bit different every so often, otherwise the villains get to know you.'

He had, however, lost none of his talent for repartee. In the Club Row on a Sunday morning he needs it, for this is one of the surviving fragments of nineteenth-century London.

Not that there is much of the kind of robust warmth that goes with cockney tradition. Club Row has a sort of pinched feeling about it, an atmosphere of meanness. Properly known as Sclater Street, E.C., it consists of a narrow strip of stalls and shops running off Bethnal Green High Street. Once it was entirely devoted to the wild bird trade, then to pets in general, now to anything you care to think of. In Club Row on a Sunday morning nowadays you can buy anything from a puppy to a football, from a plastic bag of goldfish to pop records and candy floss.

As the Inspector responsible for the East End, John Kenny patrols Club Row most weeks: because it is an area where Inspectors tradition-ally go in pairs, other London Inspectors share the duty on a rota. Most of the time, he said, it wasn't a question of actually bringing prosecu-tions, but of simply being there. Because he is there, the traders will be more cautious. 'If I do see a bird I know's been trapped, then I take it away, and report the whole case to RSPCA Headquarters.'

'Supposing the trader objects?'

'Then I'd get a policeman. He'd take him down to Bethnal Green

Inspector Kenny in Club Row, *above and opposite.*

police station and charge him under Section 12 of the Wild Birds Act. They've got pictures and charts of all the wild birds down there at the nick, for identification.'

Why do the Club Row traders go to such lengths to capture wild goldfinches and linnets? One reason is the East Ender's favourite hobby of keeping song-birds. When Marie Lloyd sang her famous song about her old cock linnet, she was celebrating what was even in the eighteen-nineties, a time-honoured tradition. Nowadays, because people are often not allowed to keep dogs and cats in high-rise flats, the bird trade is more flourishing than ever. In Club Row a linnet will sell for up to £1, though a good singer will fetch much more. In 1972 the Society made 157 successful prosecutions over bird trapping. A

realistic estimate of the total number trapped would be nearer 20,000.

Most prosecutions are under the Protection of Birds Act of 1933, presented in the House of Commons by the novelist John Buchan. The Act made it illegal to trap any of sixty-six species of birds, including thrushes, robins, linnets, most kinds of finches, and many other song-birds. On the principle that a bird that had never known its freedom would not miss it, the Act made it legal to breed from those already in captivity.

Kenny explained that a bird that is aviary-bred must be close-ringed – that is, it must have had a ring put round its leg within five days of birth, though the trappers can get round this by forcing the rings on to the legs of a bird caught in a wild state.

Was it true, I asked, that trappers would sometimes blind a bird to make it sing better? Kenny said they did blind them, not usually to make them sing better, but to use them as decoys. 'They use hot needles or acid from car batteries. I've never come across one of them, thank God. Because if I did, I'd thump his head in.'

I went with Kenny into a pet shop where the proprietor said there was nothing he minded us seeing. It was a gloomy, rather ill-smelling place with a heap of small dead tropical birds that one of the staff said had died in transit. Kenny ignored these, but took a good look at two birds the pet-shop owner said were Indian wagtails.

'I reckon they're British wagtails, but you've got to be so careful.' We worked our way back up the market to the railway arches where old, expressionless men in chokers were selling puppies. The puppies were small and white and bumbling, like puppies in a cartoon.

'That's a beautiful dog', said the stallholder without a flicker. 'A real aristocrat. None of your Club Row rubbish.'

We went into the café opposite: it was full of people drinking cups of tea and reading Sunday papers. Presently Kenny looked up. 'There's something in here,' he said. 'I'm sure I can hear a redpoll.'

What with the din of clattering cups and the chatter, I thought he was joking, but he wasn't. 'There's something there! They'll keep them in anything, little bags in their trousers, or loose in their pockets.'

A rather swarthily good-looking young man came over and asked Kenny in a friendly way if he'd nicked anyone lately, then said he had something private to tell him. When he had gone Kenny said he was a trader he had recently done for an £85 fine for trapping. Now the young man had come to tip him off about a sale that was going to happen in the pub on the corner of Club Row the following Saturday evening.

'You mean he's shopping the other trappers?'

'I suppose he thinks it's someone else's turn.' John Kenny grinned reflectively. 'Though I will say for him, he looks after his birds. All the birds we took off him were well-cared for.'

Outside, in Club Row the pet stalls were beginning to pack up, Kenny and the other Inspector began to look active. 'This is the time I like to be about. You get a lot of these villains'll leave the puppies on the pavement.'

'The ones they haven't sold?' I looked across to one of the stalls. There were half a dozen puppies still tumbling around the barrow.

'They'll just leave them on the pavement', repeated Kenny with anger. 'To be collected by the dustman. Only they won't, not so long as I'm here. The other thing I've got to look out for are the pigeons.'

'Pigeons?'

'When the market finishes they come down because of all the straw that gets left lying about – then the yobbos go for them with sticks. Last week I had an injured pigeon in one hand and a yobbo in the other. He got away, but the police and I followed the gang down all the back streets. I don't think they'll come back in a hurry.'

I said goodbye to John Kenny and got in the car, glad to leave Club Row behind me.

*

When I knocked at the door of the Animal Homes Department at Horsham, the face of the man at the desk looked familiar. Not surprisingly: Captain W. E. Robinson, known throughout the Society as Robbie, has been on television more than forty times. As head of the Animals Homes Department he recently did a whole series on Thames Television with Eamonn Andrews. Called *Give a Pet a Home*, the idea was that animals in need of homes were shown, the care of them explained, and letters from would-be owners asked for. After one programme in which Robbie appeared with an Alsatian, the Society received over 2,000 letters. Only one family could get the dog, but all the other applicants received a letter telling them when and where, if they wanted to give a home to an unwanted dog, RSPCA homes were open.

What really is the role of the Animal Homes Department? Robbie Robinson, an engaging character in his mid-forties who has kept a good deal of dash from his days in the Royal Marines, explained that the Department's immediate function was to run its own four animal homes. Three of these, primarily for cats and dogs, are in the Home Counties. The fourth, for horses only, is at Ningwood in the Isle of Wight.

Among other Ningwood horses are twenty or so retired from the Household Cavalry. Not long ago a reporter from the *Daily Mirror* found that former Household Cavalry horses were being sold to an abattoir in London for slaughter at £60 each. The Society got the Ministry of Defence to agree to sell them for £1 each, and now they end their days at Ningwood. If there is such a thing as class distinction in the animal kingdom, there must be some interesting social contrasts. Along with twenty or so Household Cavalry horses accustomed to strutting up and down the Mall, there are still a few pit-ponies, of which the last are likely to be retired from the mines in 1974.

Remembering Ralph Hodgson's famous poem, I asked Robbie if the pit-ponies were often in bad shape? They were, he said, nearly always in super shape. 'The average pit-pony's better looked after than one in the average children's riding school. You never see them blind nowadays. They do get killed sometimes, but so do miners.'

The Department's wider role is to advise the branches. If a branch needs planning permission to build an Animal Centre, or wants designs for one, these will be arranged through the Department. Thanks to the highly enlightened Animal Homes Committee, Robbie said, over the last ten years the standards of design, hygiene and general appearance have notably improved. The new catteries installed at the Southridge animal home, for instance, are regarded by vets as the most up-to-date in Europe. Runs are designed so that the cats can see other cats, but never actually touch them, thus ruling out the risk of cat-flu. Another recent advance is the rule that all dogs taken into an

The animal home at Chobham (*below and opposite*) is one of the best designed in Europe.

RSPCA home nowadays must be inoculated. 'In the past', says Robbie, 'people could say "don't get a dog from a dog's home because it might have distemper". Now, we can say an RSPCA dog is more free from disease than any.'

A New Place for Pickles

One of the happiest stories I came across was from the Animal Home at Chobham. I had already been along to Chobham and met Terry

Weekes, the friendly young ex-policeman who supervises ponies, cats and dogs in an atmosphere of green fields, white railings, and some of the most up-to-date British kennels.

Soon after my visit Terry rang me up. A few days before, he said, a Shetland pony had been brought in by the Slough Inspector. Found abandoned near London Airport, it was in a state of near-starvation and had some severe abrasions where it had probably injured itself on barbed wire. The pony had been christened Pickles. Pickles had been shown on one of the Thames Television programmes, and viewers prepared to give him a home had been asked to write in. The result had been two or three hundred letters. Now the question was who was going to get him?

'I know where I'd like it to go', said Terry Weekes. 'We've had an application from the National Children's Home, at Hildenborough in Kent. It's one of their schools for educationally subnormal children.'

'So what are you going to do?' Terry, I knew, has a handicapped child himself, and spends a lot of his leisure time helping other children similarly handicapped. If the Hildenborough school had anything like the proper facilities for a Shetland pony, there wouldn't be much doubt about where he would want it to go.

The animal home at South Godstone (*below and opposite*).

'I'm going over there tomorrow to have a look. If we do let them have the pony, would you like to see him arriving?'

Naturally I said I would. Two days later I had another call from Terry Weekes. He had been to Hildenborough, had a look round, and the facilities were even better than he had hoped for. 'They've got fields of their own and proper fencing. And Mr. Jones, the headmaster, knows about horses – he's a farmer's son himself. We're taking the pony over there tomorrow, round about eleven.'

Next morning I set off for Hildenborough. Mr. Jones turned out to be a tall and twinkling Welshman. They had already got quite a lot of animals at the school, he explained – rabbits, goats, sheep, and hamsters. When he had seen Pickles on television he had practically leapt to the telephone, got on to the RSPCA, and to his great delight had a call back from Mr. Weekes two days later.

I asked how many children were being cared for in the school. There were, Mr. Jones said, around thirty children, most of them slow learners, and many of them also maladjusted. 'When you look at some of the backgrounds they come from, it's a miracle they're as good as they are '

While we were waiting for Terry Weekes he took me round the school grounds. There were a few acres of fields, beautifully fenced, and a lot of building work going on where new classrooms were being put up to augment the existing school house. This, he said, would mean that the number of children at the school would soon be more than doubled. Also, which would come in useful for Pickles, the contractors had said they would try to leave behind the builders' huts, which would make admirable stabling.

By now the children were coming out for morning break. A few had obvious handicaps, but most looked cheerful, normal children. Soon we were surrounded by almost the whole school, for everyone had come to see the pony, and now, as we watched, a cheer went up. An RSPCA horse box swung round the drive, and a cheerful-looking Terry Weekes got out. The next moment he was leading out a brown and white Shetland pony, no bigger than an average-sized St. Bernard.

What happened next was not much less than an explosion. Perhaps the children were less inhibited than most, but for the next ten minutes there was something as near to pure joy as you can imagine.

'Can we learn to ride him? Can we keep the bridle? Could we make a little cart?'

Yes, they could, said Mr. Jones. It would be a good project, when they got the new workshop going.

Meanwhile Terry Weekes was walking the pony round, a glow on his face that matched the children's. Somebody said the pony was even prettier than he had been on television, then suddenly came a note of discord.

'Can I kick the pony?' The speaker was a small, cheerful-looking little lad who Mr. Jones had pointed out earlier as coming from a background that was, he told me, hair-raising.

'Do you think he deserves kicking, James?' Mr. Jones smiled. It was a very Welsh smile, very commanding, very gentle. For a moment I wondered what James was going to say, but he said nothing, only ran and sank his head on Mr. Jones's elbow. The other children watched, and you felt they watched with comprehension.

When I walked back to the school buildings afterwards with Mr. Jones I asked him whether James would really have kicked the pony.

'I think he might, if he got the chance. That's why I wouldn't let him near it. Not for a long time yet.'

Presently we stopped again to watch the pony, which was still trotting round, with one of the children leading him. Over by the fence Terry Weekes was talking to the two boys who would be looking after Pickles. Both, said Mr. Jones, had come from difficult homes. 'The thing is, that one wants to be a farmer. Looking after the pony's going to be a tremendous help for that boy.'

'Could it eventually do something for James?'

'It could.' Mr. Jones considered, then said it would have to be a long time yet for the pony's sake, but that learning to care for animals could produce extraordinary results.

'Is it a question of learning to love something?'

'I wouldn't say it was primarily love. The point I make to them is that an animal has rights of its own. We've got a dog at the school. He's an incredibly good-tempered dog, but I tell them that there may be times when the dog doesn't want to be petted and cuddled. The dog has rights, and they must learn to respect them.'

Very often too, Mr. Jones said, the animals could be a sort of refuge. 'When a child's decided he hates humans, you'll often find him holding a rabbit and scowling at the world. One of the most remarkable cases we had here was a boy called Steve. Steve came here with a violent reaction to everyone – he was a petrified, pathetic creature, almost frightened of his own shadow. He couldn't accept any form of rebuke or criticism. He'd simply want to hit you.

'We didn't have a lot of animals then, but we had a goat. One day the boy who'd been looking after the goat left, and Steve began to take it over. He looked on that goat as his refuge – if he'd had a stormy interlude with his housefather he'd disappear, and we'd always know where to find him. He'd be down there with the goat. Sitting in the hay with his arms around it. Slowly he began to realize that there was a living creature that needed him, and from there on, he started to be better. Once he'd found he could make a relationship with an animal, he could move on and make relationships with humans. Later we put him in charge of other animals, and he reared several sets of lambs. Today that boy's doing very well. He's one of our successes.'

Night Call at Harmsworth

One place where any sick animal would be lucky to get taken is the Harmsworth Animal Hospital in North London. A large modern building just off the Seven Sisters Road, the Hospital has some of the most sophisticated veterinary equipment in the country. Basically, the service is meant for people who cannot afford vets' fees. Anyone arriving will be asked if they can afford to pay. If it appears they can, they will be referred to the nearest vet. If not, their animal will get some of the best veterinary treatment in London for nothing, or if they choose, a small donation.

What sort of people really need free treatment for their pets? Typical of the kind of person Harmsworth is meant for is Mr. O'Malley, an elderly Irishman who came into the afternoon surgery when I was there. With him he brought an enormous cat called Timmy who was, he said, a bit run down.

David Grant, the vet on duty, eyed what appeared to be a magnificent specimen of a cat, and said that if that was what he was like when he was run down, he'd like to see him when he wasn't.

All the same, said Mr. O'Malley, the cat had been sick rather a lot and had been bleeding from his eyes.

Mr. Grant ran an expert hand over various bits of Timmy's anatomy, then opened his mouth. 'It's his teeth that are the trouble. No wonder he's run down with teeth like that.'

While he was examining Timmy's teeth I talked to Mr. O'Malley. He was rather a handsome old man, with a touch of dignity about him that didn't quite conceal the shortcomings of the old-age pension. Until a couple of years back, he told me, he had worked on the railway, and in the days when he was earning, he'd have been glad to pay for the cat's treatment. Now he was alone in the world except for his two cats: if he had had to pay for them at the vet, it would have meant going without something. At the same time, he said, he couldn't bear to see one of his cats ill. 'I'm not religious', he said, with a certain splendid disregard for logic, 'but I believe God put everything in this world to live.'

Meanwhile David Grant had finished looking at the cat. What Mr. O'Malley had better do, he said, was bring Timmy back on Thursday and they would fix a dental session. After they had both gone I asked what the treatment would cost. 'A full dental treatment like that would cost £6, or maybe £7', said David. 'Mr. O'Malley's the sort of person that we're here for.'

Another side of the work at Harmsworth is the round-the-clock emergency service. If an accident is reported at any time during the night the call will go to a Casualty Centre at the front of the building.

What sort of emergency calls does the night service get? Mr. Henry Hunt, the manager on duty, turned out to be the doyen of the service. A leonine-looking figure with a voice like an Edwardian actor, he had, he said, been with the Society forty years and was due to retire next year. Yes, he supposed, he had quite a few stories but the trouble now was that he wouldn't have time to tell me many because the phones were starting to get busy. For a start the ambulance driver and Mr. Grant, the vet, were just going out to Golders Green to rescue a dog that had got itself stuck underneath a shed.

'Does the vet always go out on night calls?'

Mr. Hunt explained that the vet was on duty till ten o'clock. 'As long as he's on duty, and if it looks as though he may be needed. In this case the dog may need to be anaesthetized before he can be rescued.'

Meanwhile Tom, the ambulance driver, was looking up the quickest way to get to Golders Green. Mr. Hunt observed with the voice of experience that at this time of day it could take three-quarters of an hour, then went back to talking to someone on one of his two phones: it was a lady who had found an injured bird in her back garden.

'What part of London are you speaking from, my dear? Upper Holloway? Is it possible' – he stressed it with immense courtesy – 'for someone to bring it in, my dear?'

It seemed that it was possible. Mr. Hunt went on to deal rather briskly with someone else who wanted to know what you did with a cat that couldn't learn to be house-trained. ('It's only a question, my dear, of patience and persuasion. There's no other method.') A cheerful West Indian came to the window to collect a dog called Susie: in the early evening the Casualty Centre also deals with animals that have been treated in the hospital itself. No, said Mr. Hunt, there was no charge, but if the West Indian would care to give a donation, it would be very welcome.

After that there came a slight lull, except for a call from a lady inquiring about a missing dog. 'I wouldn't give up hope, my love, I'd get in touch with Battersea. You can't do more, I'm afraid', said Mr. Hunt.

In the lull I asked him what sort of calls came in during the middle of the night? Mostly, he said, they were accidents. Someone would ring in to report an animal run over or lying in the street. When that happened the ambulance driver would go and either painlessly destroy it or bring it in. A lot of the calls came from the police, or from the fire brigade.

Sometimes, he said, the accidents were more unusual. Not long ago one of the drivers had had to let himself down by a rope from the viaduct at Highgate Archway, rescuing a pigeon that had got its foot trapped. Another time Mr. Hunt had had a call to a nightclub in Mayfair that had an ornamental pond. 'They kept a few terrapins and a small crocodile. What happened was that the crocodile had got one of the terrapins stuck in its jaw, and they wanted us to go down and release it. Fortunately, when we appeared, the crocodile opened his mouth to snap at us, and the terrapin dropped out. All the same, it was a nasty moment.'

By this time there had been quite a few more calls. One was a radio-call from Tom, the ambulance driver, to say that he and David Grant had freed the dog at Golders Green and were on their way back. I asked how many phone calls the Centre would deal with in a night: roughly, said Mr. Hunt, there would be 120, with 250 at weekends. While he was showing me the book where he noted down all calls, there came another.

This time it was from the landlord's wife at a pub in Hoxton. It seemed that the pub overlooked a patch of waste ground near the edge

of Hoxton Market. The market people used the land for storing their wheelbarrows, and now a litter of kittens had been born in one of these. Two had been savaged by a dog, and the lady from the pub's concern was how to save the others – the problem was, she said, that the gate to the waste ground was locked.

'When you say you haven't got a way of getting them out, my dear, where exactly are the kittens? If I send a driver along to you, can you show him where they are? And this is in Hoxton Street, my dear?'

Mr. Hunt put down the phone, and duly inscribed the query in the call book. 'That'll be another for Tom when he gets back.'

I said goodnight, left Mr. Hunt to his next hundred calls, and went off wondering what would happen to North London's cats and dogs without the Harmsworth.

The Harmsworth Animal Home, North London. It was visited by H.R.H. Prince Charles in 1971.

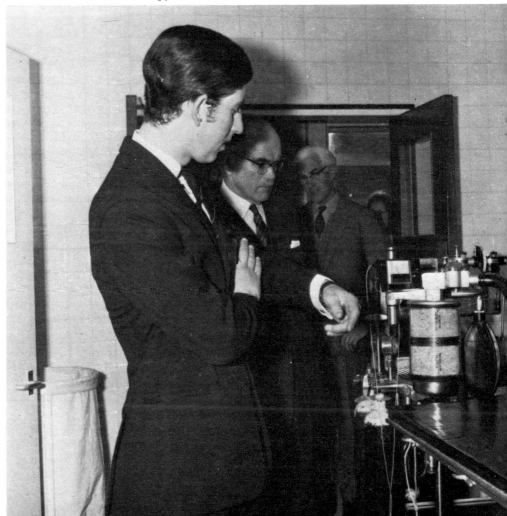

8: The Next Half-Century

A school of whales is not a coal-mine – *Konrad Lorentz*

The Farther Shores

In this book so far we have looked at various activities of the RSPCA. We have seen the work of the Inspectors and the branches: we have got some idea of how the organization works, and the range of modern problems which it faces. What we must now do is look at these problems in the broader context of the future. To begin with, what sort of influence can the RSPCA hope to have outside this country?

*

Earlier on we saw how the Society, right from its first days, had forged links with animal welfare groups in other countries. As far back as the 1860s there had been international conferences of SPCAs, meeting in places as varied as Dresden and the Crystal Palace.

Meanwhile the Society's ideals had spread to many remoter places where, in the old colonial days, there was a British influence. No account of the history of the humane movement would be complete without some reference to those redoubtable English ladies who, in Victorian times or our own, have taken pity on neglected animals from Montevideo to Malta. Often mocked to begin with, many survived to be greatly loved. Such a one was Mrs Brooke, whose husband was stationed in the army in Egypt in the 1920s. To her horror Mrs. Brooke found that many British army horses had been left in Egypt after the first World War and were pulling wagons in the streets, often badly used and overworked. She began a hospital for the abandoned horses, which still operates as one of the most efficient animal centres in Cairo. (Mrs. Brooke herself became so popular that once when her car got stuck in a narrow Cairo alley, the locals picked it up bodily and turned it the right way round.)

Sometimes, through the efforts of such exiled animal-lovers, local welfare societies have been formed. Since 1948 the Society's Overseas Department has built up links with more than fifty local groups in the Commonwealth and foreign countries. Some of these employ one, or sometimes several, Inspectors: Zambia and Trinidad, for instance, have both sent local Inspectors to the RSPCA for training. In terms of cash, the Society makes grants amounting to £14,000 a year from its Overseas Fund to help what are often small and struggling local groups. Apart from keeping up contact with overseas SPCAs and administering these grants, the Overseas Liaison Officer, Mr. Frank Gravestock deals with a constant stream of correspondence. 'It can be anything', he says, 'from working out the details of a £500 grant for a new Minivan for Majorca, to sending designs and drawings for a new cattery to the SPCA in Mauritius.' The morning I saw him he had just had a letter from a lady starting an animal welfare society in Utica Pike, near Jeffersonville, Indiana. Recently on holiday in Britain, she said, she had seen the RSPCA posters on the SELFA campaign, and wanted to know details of the Society.

Nowadays the Overseas Department's work is tending to merge increasingly with that of ISPA, the International Society for the Protection of Animals. Founded jointly by the RSPCA and the American animal welfare societies, ISPA has main offices in London, Bonn, and Boston. It is financed by more than fifty countries, whose contributions range from £20,000 each from the British and American founders to Fiji's $40. ISPA's aim is the world-wide prevention of cruelty and the relief of animal suffering. It is listed as a consultative body with the United Nations through Unesco and FAO, and also represents animal welfare interests on, for example, IATA and the International Commission on Whaling.

What can ISPA actually do in practical terms to further its aim of preventing suffering? Because of the expense involved, explains one of its London directors, Trevor Scott, ISPA decided from the beginning against scattering a few Inspectors in permanent stations overseas. 'On our resources it'd be impossible to cover more than a very few places. What we've done instead is to set up a team of commando-type Field Officers who can go anywhere, either in an emergency or on a special project.' The result is that the list of territories covered by ISPA Field Officers sounds a bit like a carve-up by world powers – one Field Officer has the Western Hemisphere, another Europe, another Africa, and so on.

Given such daunting terms of reference, what sort of achievements can ISPA actually point to? Mr. Scott told me that one of the most

Field Officer John Walsh rescues a deer during Operation Gwamba.

dramatic had been the aid given after the Peruvian earthquake in 1970. 'One Sunday afternoon I was rung up by one of our Field Officers from Boston, saying he'd been asked by the Peruvian Embassy in Washington for help. He got there so fast that he arrived ahead of the UN relief team. When they did arrive, the air-medics were so short of drugs that they used ours for the relief of humans.' For weeks after that the ISPA man and a team of locally recruited vets toured villages in the disaster area, rescuing hundreds of injured cattle, sheep and goats, and humanely killing others.

Sometimes a project designed to improve the life of people in a primitive area can mean disaster for animals. One such example came in 1964, when ISPA learned that a new hydro-electric dam was being built in Surinam. When the dam was built, it was estimated, 600 square miles of virgin rain-forest would be flooded. Two ISPA men set out immediately to reconnoitre the territory. A huge rescue operation, they saw, must be mounted if thousands of animals were not to drown. Field Officer Walsh started work with a rescue team which at one time included forty boats. For about a year he worked, often in conditions of extreme danger, rescuing animals from areas of high ground as they became slowly flooded. In the end nearly 10,000 animals, birds and reptiles were saved in what was known as Operation Gwamba.

Not all ISPA's operations arise from disasters, whether natural or man-made. Recently it co-operated with the RSPCA in demonstrations leading to the introduction of humane slaughtering in both Brazil and Greece, where previously the traditional way of slaughtering sheep and pigs was with a knife, while cattle had been killed with hammers. 'We've helped to revolutionize methods in Greek abattoirs', says Mr. Scott. 'And in Brazil our methods have become so accepted that they've now got to the stage of appointing a local agent for the manufacturers of humane killers.' In West Africa, a similar training programme recently took place, with ISPA demonstrators touring the villages and giving a training course for local SPCA Inspectors.

Ultimately ISPA's responsibility is to choose priorities from among a vast and often conflicting stream of urgent needs. 'It may sound an impossible job', says Trevor Scott, 'but what I've got to do is try to assess the depth of suffering. In 1974, for instance, we're going to have to send a team to Panama because of the new hydro-electric scheme they're building. If we don't do something, thousands of animals will die when the valleys there are flooded. They'll die because no one's all that bothered. That's where we come in. It's our job to be bothered.'

*

There is one potential side of the Society's international work which we must look at briefly. This is the project, first raised in the anniversary year, of forming a group to represent the interests of animal welfare within the European Community. Towards the end of 1973 meetings were held with animal welfare groups from various Common Market countries, with a view to setting-up a constitution for a Joint Society.

If such a new group were formed, what would be its role? John Hobhouse, the RSPCA's chairman, thinks an important part would be the setting-up of committees such as those the RSPCA has already

New methods for Greek abattoirs. An ISPA officer
demonstrates the latest humane killers.

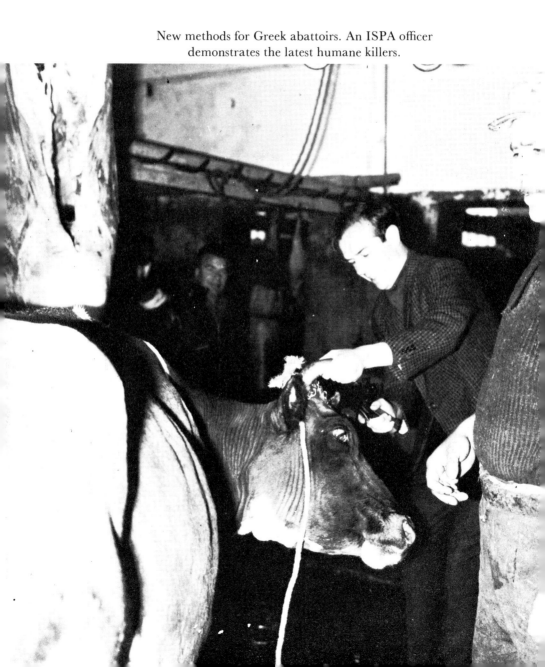

Traditional method of loading cattle in the Galapagos Islands. ISPA Officers were able to persuade the islanders to introduce more humane methods.

formed on such subjects as Farm Animals and Experimentation on Live Animals, 'The advantage would be', he says, 'that on these you'd get some of the best brains in Europe. The presence of a leading British or German scientist or vet would mean that their opposite numbers from, say, Italy or France, would be glad to join as well.'

Through such committees, Hobhouse thinks, it might eventually be possible to get the Community itself to pass laws to cover the whole of Europe. 'A law on pre-stunning is one that we and the other European societies would like to see enforced. Another would be a law insisting on adequate lairages for animals going from one country to another.' To see that the laws are observed, Hobhouse suggests with cautious optimism, the ultimate aim might be a small squad of mobile Inspectors, working on the RSPCA pattern.

If such a project does eventually get off the ground, it could clearly be one where the Society, with 150 years of accumulated expertise, could make a major contribution. Meanwhile, it is time for us to turn to another aspect of the future.

From rabbit care to clearing ponds. RSPCA Education Officers work out of doors as well as in schools and colleges.

'You get some biology teachers who spend half their time teaching respect for the environment,' says David Paterson, 'and the other half of the time they're getting their kids so desensitized they're jumping on frogs.'

As a former biology teacher himself, David Paterson should know. Before coming to the RSPCA he was head of a department of science in a comprehensive school, and also helped to start several homes for handicapped children. Now head of the Society's Education Department, he is tackling one of its most exacting but also most exciting jobs.

Education has, till recently, largely through shortage of staff and lack of funds, tended to be the Cinderella of the Society. 'Till a year or so back', says Paterson, 'the Department mostly consisted of a few people going round primary schools talking about the ethics of pet care. What we're tackling now is a whole new concept of animal welfare teaching.' Over the last two years, the Department has been re-organized and very considerably extended. Today there is a team of qualified Education Officers, working in sixteen regions of the country. Education is, after all, says the Committee Chairman, Mrs. Peggy Tait, one of the first objects of the Society. 'Our basic job is the prevention of cruelty. You can't prevent cruelty unless you educate people to treat animals properly.'

What kind of conditions must the educational programme be geared to meet in the later 1970s? In the primary schools, David Paterson sees the basic task as still being the teaching of pet care. Since 1972, the Department has brought out a whole new series of wallcharts on the care of domestic pets, ranging from cats and dogs to hamsters. The series is being augmented by such methods as project-packs for both primary and secondary schools. These contain teaching material such as films and slides with commentaries as well as cards of information for each child. New film-strips have been produced or planned, with a set of attractive-sounding titles ranging from *Creatures of the Sandy Shore* to *Amphibians, Mammals of Field and Forest*, and *Country Manners*.

It is when the child gets further on in the school, that the really important part of the teaching comes in. Take the film the Department has produced on pigs: the first section shows pigs in their traditional surroundings, then on factory farms. At various points the film breaks off to include filmed interviews with children on factory farming, aimed to spark off further discussion in the classroom. 'The thing you have to remember', says Mrs. Tait, 'is that a lot of children have seldom actually seen a pig. If we're not careful we're going to find ourselves bringing up a generation of children who've never seen a farm animal in its natural setting.' Future films will do the same for cattle, hens and sheep: another, already completed and entitled *Side by Side*, is aimed to show older school-children how they can help pensioners by caring for their pets.

Meanwhile David Paterson's main concern is that in our secondary schools many children are being, as he says, desensitized. Because new systems in biology teaching lay far more stress on practical work, even ordinary comprehensive school laboratories are beginning to resemble vivisection centres. 'You get a child who, at primary school, has learnt how to look after budgies and rabbits. He's liable to start off his work in the secondary school by dissecting a rat. At various stages from then, he'll do things that are more advanced. It's not surprising you get cases of fifth-formers killings cats or jumping on live frogs from local ponds. To me, that attitude to live things is a logical outcome of the way we teach them.' In some cases, Paterson adds, it happens that animals kept as pets have later been used for dissection in the same school's labs. In any case, he thinks, twelve is far too young for children to be taught to start dissecting.

If on the other hand a twelve-year-old needs to be taught some anatomy, is there an alternative answer? Paterson believes there is, and has persuaded six schools in Yorkshire and the south-east to carry out a pilot scheme which he hopes may be followed up throughout the country. Basically, the method is to use pre-dissected specimens, kept in preserving fluid in a glass jar. 'A specimen in a glass jar with fluid doesn't have the emotional impact of cutting up something that's just died.'

What about the cost of pre-dissected specimens? Paterson points out that the economic saving could be an important lever to persuade more schools to use this method. The average cost of a laboratory rat is £1, while pre-dissected specimens cost £8. 'Set that against the 125 rats you'd need for 250 children to do their dissection in pairs,' he says, 'and the school's saving more than £100. If we could get the dissection figure down by 25 per cent we could prevent a tremendous carnage – let alone the emotional damage done to the children.'

In many other ways the Education Department's work has come a long way from the days of essay prizes at the Crystal Palace. Probably the most significant recent development is the increasing status of the Education Officers: whereas in the old days an Education Officer would rarely get far beyond the stage of talking to primary school classes about the care of hamsters, nowadays they give regular lectures

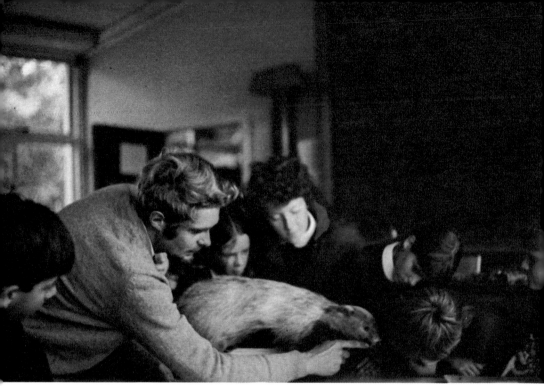

An Education Officer in the classroom.

and film shows in secondary schools and often in Teachers' Training Colleges and Universities as well. Some Education Officers have already begun to develop such close links with school authorities in their region that they are now automatically booked to lecture to future teachers. In recent years university debates, field study weekends for graduates, and film shows in secondary schools have all been mounted.

What about the junior membership of the RSPCA? Youth groups, known as Animal Defenders, are mostly based on primary schools. (Those in secondary schools are called Junior RSPCA, and share most privileges of full members.) 'The sort of thing Defender groups can do', says Mr. Paterson, 'is to make themselves responsible for clearing a hedge or field of litter. This isn't simply respect for the environment – we're concerned with litter as a hazard for animals. You get cattle swallowing plastic bags, or the ring-pull metal tops from beer-cans.' One Animal Defender group in the Forest of Dean cleared a wide area of picnic litter, including a lot of cans which ponies could have got their hooves stuck in. When another primary school group picked on a local pond and decided to keep it clear of litter, one of the

Posters for exhibition in schools. As well as issuing visual aids, the Education Department answers up to 2,000 queries a week from children.

things they picked up was ninety yards of nylon line which would have been a death trap for birds using the pond.

Few people would think of thrown-away milk bottles as a hazard to animals, but Mr. Paterson suggests this is another thing to be looked out for by Animal Defender groups. 'Stop at any lay-by on a major road', he says, 'and you're sure to find a few milk bottles thrown away behind the hedge. Each one that's been there more than a week may have as many as eight small creatures in it, voles, shrews, a couple of mice and so on. The trouble is they crawl inside, then die because they can't get out.'

Towards the Future

Apart from the Council itself, the man most likely to influence the Society's course of action over the next few years is the Executive Director, Major Ronald Seager. Seager himself was promoted to his present job from being a regional organizer in 1963. His relaxed manner conceals an instinctive grasp and forcefulness which is immediately apparent in committee. In his time as Executive Director he has helped to plan and carry out the far-reaching reforms which have led, for example, to much greater professionalism among the staff. It is also Major Seager's job to maintain the Society's contacts and good relations with other animal welfare bodies, varying from the Royal Society for the Protection of Birds to the Battersea Dogs' Home. Another highly important contact is that with the British Veterinary Association, with whom the Society keeps a continual liaison through a joint committee.

Major Seager's immediate daily work may be anything from going round to branch meetings, talking to new Inspectors, to writing letters to the Ministry of Agriculture or the press. The day I saw him he had just been writing a letter to all the national newspapers asking motorists to try to avoid hitting birds, during a fine spell of weather when more cars than usual were on the roads. 'How many motorists take any trouble to avoid them?' he says. 'It's so easy. Just by taking your foot off the accelerator.'

What aspects of the Society's work, I asked, did he see changing over the next ten years? Major Seager feels strongly that the branches should become still more involved with the work of Headquarters. As an example he quotes the branches' work for the SELFA campaign, and what they can do to help in the 1974 campaign on spaying. Another idea is that branches unable to afford an animal home of their own can get together and form a joint one – this, he told me, was already happening at Leicester and at Boreham Wood. Ultimately he would like to see something like regional boards, perhaps taking on some of the authority at the moment vested in the Council. 'This is something we've been moving slowly towards for the last few years. Till recently there was virtually no such thing as regional organization. Now we have the regional representatives on the Council, paid regional organizers working alongside them, and now the same pattern with the Education Officers.'

I asked how he felt the Inspectors' role might develop – was it going to be difficult to get the right kind of Inspectors in the future? Major Seager told me he was constantly surprised at the quality of people applying to become Inspectors. 'We're always being told that young people don't care nowadays. What's impressive is the amount of dedication in the young chaps we get applying.' On the question of pay, he said he recognized that many Inspectors found it hard to meet the rising cost of living. 'On the other hand you've got to remember he's getting his house free, which is worth probably £800 a year.' One of the innovations which Seager himself has persuaded the Council to introduce is the arrangement that a retiring Inspector can go on living rent-free in the house he is occupying at the time of retirement. On the question of leisure, he says, he felt the Inspectors had a just complaint. Seager's own answer would be to appoint a further forty Inspectors on top of the present 200, so that weekend duties could be spread more widely. 'What this amounts to is really a recruiting question. Once we can get the extra staff, I don't think there'd be much difficulty in getting the Council to approve it.'

In an age of public relations, Seager accepts that much of the Society's most valuable work will be in the sphere of campaigns on a specific theme. For the anniversary year, for example, he hopes to see a major campaign mounted on animal experimentation. At the same time he stresses that such campaigns are far more likely to succeed if they have a clear but limited aim. 'It'd be no good our going out and campaigning against experimentation in general. What I hope we shall do is go for something very specific – either the duplication of experiments, or perhaps experiments in schools.'

In planning campaigns, Seager points out, the Society must think of the cost, of the likely response from public opinion, and also whether a particular theme lends itself to publicity. 'There are campaigns', he says, 'which are politically feasible and others which are not.' Ideally, he would like to see campaigns to abolish intensive farming and ritual slaughter, but acknowledges the practical and political difficulties.

Meanwhile, he has great hopes of what the Wild Life Committee can do for British wild animals. 'Now that Lord Arran's Bill to protect the badger is through the Lords, it can only be a question of time before we get a Bill to protect the otter.' Another of the activities of the Wild Life Committee is a study on the habits of the fox. 'It could be that the findings would show the fox not to be the predator he's often thought to be. If that did happen, a lot of the arguments about fox-hunting would disappear.'

Looking to the further future, Major Seager would ideally like to see what he calls a charter of rights for all creatures. 'It may be crying for the moon,' he says, 'but ultimately some sort of minimal freedom needs to be guaranteed so that animals aren't squeezed out of existence by the pressures of urbanization, population, and pollution.' The single factor that causes him most distress in relation to animals is confinement. 'Whenever animals are reared and kept in captivity the sheer boredom and lack of any outlets for emotional and instinctive behaviour can only be regarded as suffering on a massive scale. Thousands of animals and birds are treated more as stock in trade than as living creatures.'

Might there ever come a day when kindness to animals would be taken for granted so that the need for the Society would disappear? Major Seager said that he came to the reluctant conclusion it wasn't a likely prospect. 'The number of animals exploited by man has never been higher than it is today. If Broome and Martin came back they would find far more kindness to domestic pets – but civilization has not curbed man's desire for gain. The result is that you simply get far more sophisticated techniques of exploitation.'

How, as it moves into the next half-century, can the Society combat such methods? As we have traced its story two themes, one historical and the other modern, have become more and more apparent.

Through its long history the RSPCA has become something more than a Society of people. Often its influence has been out of all proportion to its numbers. At such times – and the SELFA campaign is both the most recent and the best example – it has become a unique expression of the national conscience.

The other point we have seen gradually emerging is a more modern one. In recent years, in particular, the Society has geared itself to its aims by being far more professional and resolutely armed with facts. When cruelties are opposed, the case against them will be argued by highly expert people working from well-based research. 'When we promote a cause today', says John Hobhouse, 'we still need emotion to prime the pump. The difference is that today we also deal in indisputable facts. Since 1972 we're being listened to in Whitehall and in Parliament – which is surely where it matters?'

Back to Mallydam's Wood

'When the leaves come down, we've lost our canopy. Suddenly the wood is very open.'

I had gone back for a last look round to Mallydam's Wood. Now, on a November evening, I stood with John Goodman, the warden, looking at the bare trees and the pale pink rim of winter twilight. From the other side of the wood a fountain of sparks rose from the clearing where Tim, Mr. Goodman's assistant, was burning brushwood.

Back to Mallydam's Wood.

What sort of animals, I asked, were in the sanctuary now? Mr. Goodman said there was a badger that had been found hurt on a railway line, an owl that had a damaged wing, and a kestrel: not the one that had been there on my first visit, but another which had hit one of the power lines from the atomic station at Dungeness.

'How soon before you let it go?'

'I hope within a week or so.' Mr. Goodman led the way over to one of the big cages. Built into it was a special section with an open door – the idea of getting birds ready for release, he explained, was that you left them free to move a little farther from the cage each day. 'We've got these perching-posts where we put a bit of food. Then if a bird decides to leave the cage, it can do.' In the case of the kestrel, he said, it would probably be best to take him down to the Romney Marsh where he had come from. 'If he has difficulty in flying we'll race after him and get him back. But I'm confident he'll soon be off.'

In the enclosed part of the next cage there was a big white barn-owl that stared at us with disapproval. 'The local Inspector found Barney with a damaged wing', said Mr. Goodman. 'He's cured now, but the trouble is, he treats the cage as if it was a barn. He goes off each evening, then comes back. What I'd really like him to do is settle somewhere else, and find a mate.' We went past a larger run where a female badger was sniffing the evening air – a signalman had found her injured on a railway line, Mr. Goodman explained, and in her case there'd be a bit of a problem over the best place to release her. 'If we let her go in the Wood, she might be attacked by another badger whose territory it is. If we return her to where she was found, there's a risk of her getting on the railway line again. Releasing a wild animal may sound easy, but there are a lot of things you've got to think of.'

We moved away from the small area of runs and cages and walked towards the wood. There were no Red Admirals now, hardly a leaf left in the bare birchwoods. A few yellowhammers and chaffinches would be coming back from the open pasture where they had been all summer, said Mr. Goodman, but mostly the wood was full of sleeping things. He went over to an old chestnut stump, covered thickly with moss, and gently tapped it. 'I saw an adder here last month, sunning itself on one of the last days in October. Then I watched it go down into the gaps between the roots. If it gets down a foot or so, the ground there is never frozen . . .'

Just along the path there was one of the nesting boxes that are spread round the trees in the wood. He opened the little flap, shone his torch in, and scattered some peanuts from his pocket. Inside there was a tiny tapestry of thickly woven tendrils. 'There's a dormouse inside there.

He's wrapped himself in honeysuckle for the winter.'

On the other side of the wood Tim's bonfire was dying down. What, I asked, was the idea of clearing that particular section? This winter, John Goodman said, work would be beginning on the building of a new Field Study Centre. Since the Society had owned the wood, it had been used as an educational centre where parties of school-children could be shown an example of natural wildlife as it should be. 'With the new Field Study Centre a school group will be able to come and work here for the day. There'll be a small hall for showing films or slides, then the children will go into the wood and relate what they've seen to the real thing.' There would also, he said, be another building where biologists would be able to do their own research and filming of wildlife subjects. In another section of the Centre, children would be able to study insects and other small creatures from the wood. 'The point is that when they've studied some animal for the afternoon, they'll let it go. What we're trying to teach them above all is respect for the life around them.'

Respect – in a way, I thought, respect for all sorts and conditions of animals is what the Society is about. I thought of the great procession of animals I had seen, of the thousands of others that had come within its compass from the beginning. I thought of Cleo, pure dog, and all the other less fortunate strays, of Charlie the swan and Pickles the Shetland pony. I thought of the veal calves in their darkened pens and the tragic cargoes at the London Airport Hostel, of the Inspectors I had met and the scores of others I had not met, patrolling our streets and shores from Cumberland to Cornwall. I remembered the thousands of ordinary people working so that the great tide of animal suffering should somehow be diminished. The final distinction, I thought, was not between cruelty and kindness, but between the presence or the absence of the sense of caring. Nobody has to be kind to animals, any more than anyone has to write symphonies or poems. In the end it is the things we do not have to do that make our civilization richer.

By now the bonfire was almost out. I walked slowly back across the darkened wood with John Goodman to his house. As we came near to the lights Mrs. Goodman called out to say that Barney the owl had flown off. 'Tim saw him making for the barn just down the lane. He thinks he may have found a perch there.'

'If I take a bit of food down there, it might encourage Barney to stay.' The warden was already stuffing food into his pocket, and getting on his gumboots. 'If you don't mind, I won't see you off. Only if we can get him to settle in that barn —'

'The way he should be?' I remembered John Goodman's words at the beginning.

'The way he should be.'

After a hundred and fifty years, it is still the essence.

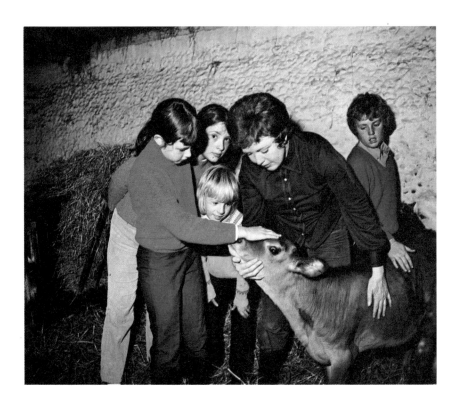

Appendixes

Royal Society for the Prevention of Cruelty to Animals

PATRONS

HER MAJESTY THE QUEEN

HER MAJESTY QUEEN ELIZABETH,
THE QUEEN MOTHER

HER ROYAL HIGHNESS PRINCESS ALICE,
COUNTESS OF ATHLONE

VICE-PRESIDENTS

The Dowager Viscountess Galway
Lord Greenwood of Rossendale, P.C., J.P.
Lieutenant-Colonel J. C. Lockwood, C.B.E., T.D., J.P.

Members of The Council of the RSPCA

The Specialist Committees

Farm Livestock Advisory Committee
Chairman: Prof. J. R. Napier, D.SC., M.R.C.S., L.R.C.P.
Secretary: P. L. Brown, Esq., B.SC., M.R.C.V.S.
Committee Members: Dr. A. R. Everton, LL.M., PH.D.
A. Fraser, Esq., M.V.SC., M.R.C.V.S., F.I.BIOL.
Sir Charles Frederick, BT., J.P.
Miss N. Gregory
Mrs. R. Harrison
Prof. P. A. Jewell, M.A., PH.D.
P. R. Lattin, Esq., M.A.
R. Meade, Esq., O.B.E.
J. Rowsell, Esq.
M. J. Pittaway, Esq., J.P., M.R.C.V.S.

Animal Experimentation Advisory Committee
Chairman: Dr. C. M. H. Pedler, M.B., B.S., PH.D., M.C.P.
Secretary: W. J. Jordan, Esq., M.V.SC., B.SC., M.R.C.V.S.
Committee Members: A. Linzey, Esq., B.D.
K. Lomas, Esq., J.P., M.P.
Richard Ryder, Esq., M.A., D.C.P., A.B.PS.S.
Prof. T. K. Ewer, B.V.SC., PH.D., M.R.C.V.S.
Conrad Latto, Esq., M.B., CH.B., F.R.C.S.
Sir Frank Fraser Darling, D.SC., PH.D., F.I.BIOL., F.R.S.E.
D. A. Paterson, Esq., M.A., F.R.S.H., M.I.BIOL.
Dr. E. T. O. Slater, C.B.E., M.A., M.B., F.R.C.P., M.R.C.V.S., D.P.M.

Wild Animals Advisory Committee
Chairman: Dr. D. M. Stoddart, B.SC., PH.D.
Secretary: W.J. Jordan, Esq., M.V.SC., B.SC., M.R.C.V.S.
Committee Members: Colonel C. L. Boyle, O.B.E.
J. M. Bryant, Esq.
Dr. M. Delaney, B.SC., M.SC., D.SC.
Lord Medway, M.A., PH.D., F.Z.S.
Prof. J. R. Napier, D.SC., M.R.C.S., L.R.C.P.
Richard Ryder, Esq., M.A., D.C.P., A.B.PS.S.
Mrs. G. A. D. Tait, M.A.

RSPCA Facts and Figures

Facilities:

59 Animal Homes	74 Clinics	102 Welfare Centres
4 Hospitals	4 Mobile Units	
221 Inspectors	36 Market Inspectors	1 Docks Inspector

Animals Treated: 1973

Clinics	125,304
Sir Harold Harmsworth Animal Memorial Hospital	26,260
Putney Hospital	13,010
Mobile Units	5,711
Headquarters' Night Staff	4,292
	174,577

Animals Humanely Destroyed:

Clinics	128,174
Sir Harold Harmsworth Animal Memorial Hospital	3,746
Putney Hospital	1,225
Mobile Units	3,737
Headquarters' Night Staff	1,665
Inspectors	101,962
	240,509

New Homes Found:

Cats	28,156
Dogs	45,997
Miscellaneous	7,062
	81,215

Animals handled at RSPCA Animal Hospital, Heathrow Airport: 815,827

Convictions obtained by The Society for Cruelty to Animals:

Complaints investigated	23,864
Verbal Cautions	3,841
Written admonitions from Headquarters	187
Offenders sentenced to imprisonment	10
Juvenile convictions	69
Persons disqualified for varying periods from keeping animals	210
Convictions	960

Associated Sister Societies

Africa

Kenya SPCA
Animal Welfare Society of Lesotho
Society for the Protection of Animals in
  North Africa
SPCA Salisbury
Cape of Good Hope SPCA
Durban and Coast SPCA
East London (SA) SPCA
Pietermaritzburg SPCA
South African Federation of SsPCA
Swaziland SPCA
Kitwe–Kalulushi SPCA
Ndola SPCA

Canada

Canadian SPCA
Canadian Federation of Humane
  Societies
Ontario Humane Society

Caribbean

Bahamas Humane Society
Bermuda SPCA
Jamaica SPCA
Trinidad and Tobago SPCA

Europe

Guernsey SPCA
Jersey SPCA
Manx SPCA
Ulster SPCA
Oslo SPCA
Sociedade Protectora Dos Animals
  (Lisbon)

Far East

SPCA Australian Capital Territory
Burnie (Tasmania) SPCA
Devonport (Tasmania) SPCA
RSPCA New South Wales
Royal Queensland Society for Preven-
  tion of Cruelty
South Australia RSPCA
Tasmania SPCA (Northern Division)
Ulverstone (Tasmania) SPCA
RSPCA (Victoria)
Western Australia RSPCA
The Animals' Welfare and Protection
  Association (Ceylon)
Ceylon Animal Protection Society
Fiji SPCA
Kobe (Japan) SPCA
Mauritius SPCA
Royal Federation of New Zealand
  SsPCA Inc
Waikato (NZ) SPCA
Wellington SPCA
Papua and New Guinea SPCA
Selangor SPCA

Mediterranean

Cyprus Animal Welfare Fund
Société Pour la Défense Des Animaux
  (Nice)

Acknowledgements

Mr. Moss's book *Valiant Crusade* (London: Cassell, 1961) is mentioned in the Preface and I am indebted to the RSPCA, the author, and the publishers for permission to quote from it. I must thank Mrs. Ruth Harrison and Messrs. Robinson and Watkins for permission to quote from *Animal Machines*, published by Vincent Stuart in 1964. The earlier history of the Society by E. G. Fairholme and Wellesley Pain, *A Century of Work for Animals* (London: John Murray, 1924) has been a most valuable source. On the story of the animal welfare movement as a whole, E. S. Turner's *All Heaven in a Rage* (London: Michael Joseph, 1964) is not only an instructive but also a delightfully written guide, which I have found most helpful. The story of the little dog Robot's discovery of the Lascaux Caves is fully told in Professor Glyn Daniel's *The Hungry Archeologist in France* (London: Faber, 1963) where I first came across it. I am also most grateful to Mr. Leslie Hicks for allowing me to make use of his own account of the *Torrey Canyon* seabirds, *At Man's Door the Crime*.

Photo credits

I am most grateful to the RSPCA for allowing me to use photographs which are their copyright, many of which have been specially taken for this book. I must also thank the National Portrait Gallery for permission to reproduce the Sir Thomas Lawrence painting of William Wilberforce; *Punch*, for the cartoon by Sir Bernard Partridge; and the BBC, for allowing me to use the two photographs on page 34. I am especially grateful to the Scottish Society for the Prevention of Vivisection for their help with photographs of animal experiments, and for permission to reproduce those on pages 154 and 156. The International Society for the Protection of Animals allowed me to reproduce two photographs, and I am also grateful to Astraka/ Wildlife Limited for the picture of Virginia McKenna and Bill Travers. Mrs. Ruth Harrison allowed me to use three photographs of factory farming, which are her copyright. The three photographs on pages 121 and 122 originally appeared in the *News of the World*, to whom I am most grateful for permission to include them here; also to Brenard Press Limited for two photographs taken at the London Airport Hostel. I must also thank the following for allowing me to reproduce photographs which are their copyright: Camera Press Limited; Dodd's Photographic Service, Bootle, Lancashire; George Ellis, Bodmin, Cornwall; *The Daily Express*; *The Kent & Sussex Courier*; *The Kentish Express*; Keystone Press Agency Limited; *The London Evening News*; *The Daily Mail*; John Mounfield, Warrington, Lancashire; *The Reading Evening Post*; Richards Brothers, Penzance; Syndication International Limited; *The Daily Telegraph*; and Topic/ Thomson Newspapers Limited.

Index

Index

Coleridge, Hon. Stephen, his views on fox-hunting, 82
Coleridge, Samuel Taylor, 100
Cope, Mrs. Angela, 75, 77; her work on Council, 78
Crowe, Revd. Henry, 81, 150
Council of RSPCA, membership and work of, 77–81, 79, 218; and Reform Group, 83–6; and SELFA campaign, 115; and Inspectorate, 209

Daily Mirror, 135, 160, 185
Dartmoor, 171
Darwin, Charles, and the Society, 27; and *Origin of Species*, 28, 150, 154
Davies, Jill, 99
Derby Branch, 99
Descartes, 7, 149
Destructions, 52–5; 93–4
Dogs, in Poplar, 62–5; in Liverpool, 86–95; in East Cornwall, 96–7; in Windsor, 98–9; experiments on, 153; rescue attempt of, 166–70; in Club Row, 184
Dowding, Lady, 157
Dowding, Lord, 96

East Cornwall Branch, 95–8
Education, in nineteenth century, 26–7; Committee, 204; Department, 204–8
Edwards, Aubrey and Maureen, 97–8
Edwards, John, owner of Bonzo, 166–70
Elmy, Inspector Gerry, his rescues, 162–70; *163*
Erskine, Lord, *11*, 12

Factory farming, development of, 141–9; possibility of campaign on, 209
Farm Livestock Advisory Committee, setting up of, 80, 147; work and effects of, 148–9; 219
Forestry Commission, 169–70

Forward, Superintendent Henry, and rescues on Dartmoor, 171
Fox-hunting, 81–6, 210
Fund-raising, 71–3, 96, 101–4

Gardner, Chief Inspector Ralph, his work for seabirds, 174–80
George IV, 13, 16
Giraffes, 5, 140
Goodman, John, xi–xii, 211–14
Gosney, Ivy, and Liverpool cats, 92–3
Grant, David, 192–4
Guardian, The, 146, 157
Gwamba, Operation, *198*, 199

Hamilton, Innes, 98–9
Hammond, Celia, and Reform Group, 85; and a seal hunt, 157–61
Hare-coursing, 109
Harmsworth Animal Hospital, filming at, 104; description of, 191–5
Harper, Rex and Julie, and seabirds, 180
Harrison, Ruth, and factory farming, 144–9
Hicks, Leslie, 177–9
Hobhouse, John, Chairman of Council, 77, 78–80; sets up specialist committees, 80; and branches, 81; and SELFA, 105–15; and Common Market, 200–2; and Parliament, 210
Houghton, Douglas, *79*, 155
Horses, conditions in nineteenth century; 28; trade to continent in, 29, *33*; wearing funeral plumes, 32; and gypsies, 66–70; export from Ireland of, 80
Hull, Animal Home at, 67, 69
Humane killers, *31*, 199
Hunt, Henry, interview with, 192–5
Hutchinson, Inspector John, 60

IATA, 132, 197
Inspectors, and appointment of first, 17; in a fight at Hanworth, 22; rescues by, 36–41, 162–70;

role and activities of, 41–2; working day of, 43–4; and the law, 45; and prosecutions, 47–9; and destructions, 52–5; qualities required by, 58; criticisms of, 60; in East End of London, 62; and Yorkshire, 65–70; and Airport Hostel, 135; and Lynmouth floods, 171; and seabirds, 174–80; in Club Row, 181–5; salaries and recruitment of, 209
ISPA, 197–9

Jacobs, David, *76*, 77
Jermyn Street, 27, *28*
Jordan, Bill, *79*, 138–41

Kenny, Inspector John, and a dog in Poplar, 62–5; in Club Row, 181–5, *182*, *183*

Lascaux, cave paintings at, 1–3
Lawless, Maureen, 123
Legal Department, 45, 73
Lions, 139–40
Liverpool, history and description of branch at, 86–95
London Airport Hostel, story of, 126–36
Lucky, rescue of cow called, 36–41
Lynmouth floods, 171

Mallydam's Wood, xi; in winter, 211–12; Field Study Centre at, 213
Maltby, Brian, *90*, 93–5
March of Concern, 103, *104*
Martin, Richard, character of, 12–13; *14*; introduces first Parliamentary Bill, 14–16; attends meeting at Old Slaughter's, 17; and Bill Burns, 18; music hall song about, 19; dies at Boulogne, and an elegy of, 20
Maynard, Inspector Geoffrey, and rescue at Scarborough, 36–41
Meade, Richard, 77, 84

Midweek, 116–19
Milner, Travelling Superintendent Frank, interview with, 65–70
Monkeys, 131, 140; experiments on, 154
Montaigne, 8
Moss, A. W., quoted, 6, 8, 22, 24

Napier, Professor John, chairs Farm Livestock Advisory Committee, 80; interview with, 147–9
National Children's Home, and a pony, 188–91
NSPCC, the Society's help in founding, 24, 26
Nerina, Nadia, 77; and Gala Performances, 78
News of the World, 121–4
Ningwood, horses' home at, 185–6

Oakes, Gordon, and a Parliamentary Bill, 97
Old Slaughter's Coffee House, *15*, 16–17
Olley, Mrs. Lilian, 71–2
Overseas Committee, 78; and Department, 197

Parliamentary Liaison Department, 73, 109
Paterson, David, interview with, 204–8
Pease, Joseph, and a Parliamentary Bill, 21, 28, 109
Pedler, Dr. Kit, and Animal Experimentation Committee, *79*, 155
Pepys, Samuel, sees an experiment, 149–50
Pickles, story of a pony called, 187–91
Pigs, on factory farms, 146
Pine-Coffin, Peter, 99
Piper, Inspector, dies after battle with cock-fighters, 22
Pit-ponies, 28, 186
Plutarch, 5
Porphyry, 5
Prosecutions, 45, 47–9, 62, 66–7
Poultry, on factory farms, 144–6